Best
Pub Walks
in South Staffordshire

Chris Rushton & Les Lumsdon

Published by Sigma Leisure – an imprint of
Sigma Press, 1 South Oak Lane, Wilmslow, Cheshire SK9 6AR, England.

British Library Cataloguing in Publication Data
A CIP record for this book is available from the British Library.

ISBN: 1-85058-361-7

Typesetting and Design by: Sigma Press, Wilmslow, Cheshire.

Cover photograph: The Fox, at Marston (Chris Rushton)

Photographs: Chris Rushton

Maps: Jeremy Semmens

Printed by: MFP Design and Print

Contents

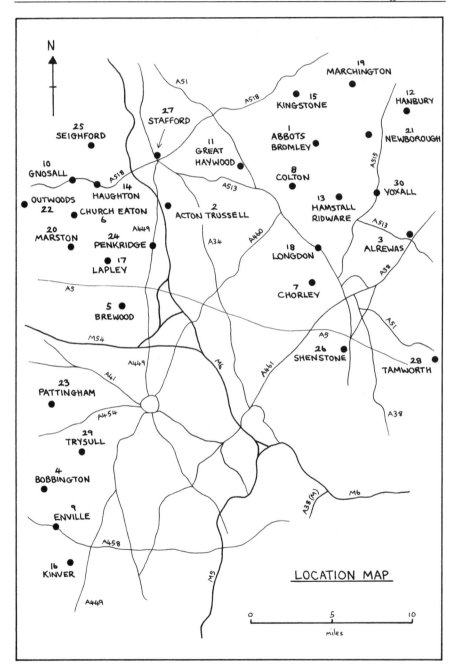

N

19 MARCHINGTON

A51

A518

15 KINGSTONE

12 HANBURY

27 STAFFORD

25 SEIGHFORD

1 ABBOTS BROMLEY

21 NEWBOROUGH

11 GREAT HAYWOOD

A515

10 GNOSALL

A518

8 COLTON

14 HAUGHTON

A513

30 YOXALL

OUTWOODS 22

CHURCH EATON 6

13 HAMSTALL RIDWARE

ACTON TRUSSELL

2

A449

3 ALREWAS

A513

20 MARSTON

24 PENKRIDGE

A34

A460

18 LONGDON

A38

17 LAPLEY

A5

7 CHORLEY

5 BREWOOD

A5

A51

M54

A449

26 SHENSTONE

28 TAMWORTH

23 PATTINGHAM

A41

A461

M6

A454

A38

29 TRYSULL

4 BOBBINGTON

A38(M)

M6

9 ENVILLE

A458

16 KINVER

M5

LOCATION MAP

A449

0   5   10

miles

Introduction

Only a decade ago, there were very few walking books about Staffordshire and nor did the county have much to commend itself in terms of the choice of small breweries. The position is different now. There are over a dozen walking books featuring all or parts of the county and fortunately it is home to a number of enterprising small breweries. They have survived under the shadows of the giants from Burton-upon-Trent and this must be good news for the discerning drinker. More will be said about this topic later, but firstly, a note about the county itself.

Staffordshire Countryside

Staffordshire's beauty lies in its variety. It is long county stretching from the moorlands of the Southern Peak to Kinver Edge. Not only are there rich river valleys such as the Blithe, Sow, Stour and Trent, but the woodland walks of Cannock Chase and the gently undulating pastures of the south and west. The south of the county is the focus of this book for it is a companion to Pub Walks in North Staffordshire completed earlier in the 1990s. Together, they introduce the casual walker to some excellent rambles but also to some of the loveliest country pubs around.

Vale of Trent

To be truthful, the book covers an area which is best described as South Staffordshire and the Vale of Trent. Take an imaginary line from Newport in Shropshire to Stafford and extend it to Uttoxeter in East Staffordshire and there you have the divide. It is purely arbitrary for in the county the change from the north to south is imperceptible. To the east of Lichfield and Tamworth the land is flatter and arable farming dominates. This is less appealing to most walkers but elsewhere the landscape is a mix of parkland, gently rising edges and rich farmland. It is ideal territory for short walks before or after lunch, or of an early evening in summer.

It is partly the natural history of an area which appeals such as the wayside lanes bedecked with campion, speedwort, vetch or perhaps cow parsley, the fox and badger, or herons taking wing from parkland pools. The heathlands of Staffordshire are important too, places like Highgate Common near Kinver, for these are home to increasingly rare reptiles.

It is also the social and industrial history that has an equal fascination for the walker. It is evident in older buildings, such as the tannery, brewery and nail-maker's shop, for example. There are also the transport networks of old, the canals and railways as well as the cartways of the past centuries. Staffordshire is rich in these highways of old, running as they do between village and town.

Staffordshire Villages

The walks invariably start in Staffordshire villages, some being much underrated. This does not mean that great attractions such as Shugborough or Weston halls, and museums such as the Ancient High House in Stafford or Stafford Castle are not to be visited. They are worth the journey but, for the walker, roadside features, earthworks on the landscape, the manor farmsteads and Georgian brick of the townhouses are the very attractions which bring life to a ramble. In this respect, Staffordshire is a storehouse waiting to be discovered.

The Staffordshire Way

Some of the walks featured either use or cross The Staffordshire Way. This long distance footpath created by Staffordshire County Council stretches from Mow Cop in the north to Kinver in the south, some 92 miles. Fortunately, in 1995 several Ramblers' groups in association with the county council undertook a survey and improvement work as part of a Jubilee Anniversary project. The result has been better waymarking, improvements to stiles and bridges and an accommodation leaflet for those taking a break on the route.

The Staffordshire Way is a very useful asset for accessing the countryside in South Staffordshire especially from Penkridge, Codsall and Kinver. It makes for an ideal day's walking.

A choice of routes at Kinver

The Walks

The walks chosen for this book are mainly from 3 to 5 miles and mostly are easy going. This is, after all, a pub walks book so the pub is as important as the walk. The walks have been chosen in some instances to open up areas which are not well walked such as Marston or Outwoods where we found obstructions, all of which have all been reported to the county council for clearance. It is a completely different story in other parts where the parish council has taken an interest in local paths, such as in Kinver. Here, local people can be justifiably proud of the excellent condition of the footpath network.

Perception is a difficult subject in that when we walked the paths our notes about features stand out in our minds rather than yours! You will, no doubt, find minor annoyances when following a route for this very reason. Some of these will not be of the authors' making but we beg your forgiveness for those that are! What was once a grassy path last year might be overgrown this, or could easily become a tractor track. The instructions should, however, be sufficient to guide you through the walks without any other help despite changes which are likely to occur.

Many find a map useful, however. Our recommendation is to use Pathfinder maps as the detail allows field by field checking of a path. The maps can become dated, in that woods are felled and old barns converted to cottages, or new roads created. Nevertheless, they are the best for the walker.

If you do find problems with the walks then please let us know by way of the publisher or better still report all crop and other obstructions to the Rights of Way Officer, Staffordshire County Council, Martin Street, Stafford. Sometimes, when a path becomes popular due to its inclusion in a book, we receive correspondence saying that barbed wire has been placed on a stile, 'bulls in field' notices have appeared, and other devices to deter the casual walker. This is a pity for, while rights of way were working ways in the past, they remain part of a transport network of the future based on leisure and recreation. You have a right to use them! This might sound rather obvious but, every time a selfish landowner obstructs a path by way of a crop or wire it takes time, money and resources to have it cleared. More sensible landowners realise that easy-to-use and well-marked paths avoid trespass and ensure that walkers pass by without fuss.

Public Transport

As you know, walking and drinking go well together but not drinking and driving. The authors endorse the Countrygoer concept wherever possible, i.e., using local buses and trains into the countryside to minimise impact on the environment and to help local communities retain a much-needed facility. One of the main problems is getting up to date information. In Staffordshire it could not be easier: simply 'phone STAFFORDSHIRE BUSLINE on 01785 223344 or 01543 577099 for details of local buses. For rail enquiries anywhere in the country you can also 'phone the national enquiry number on 0345 484950.

The Pubs

Admittedly, the walk has to be good to entice most of us out but a homely pub makes it even better. One of life's joys is to be able to call into a good old English country pub after a day's walking. It nearly beats having a good soak in the bath after a ramble! Many of the inns of Staffordshire were built originally as roadside houses, established to serve the needs of coach travellers before the advent of the railway. Some came with the canal era and others grew up as homebrew ale houses during the Victorian days of industrial growth.

Those days have long since gone and the pubs of the 1990s are those built near major road interchanges as eating houses or as large estate pubs. The rural pub has been hard-pushed to survive. Many have now gone, forced into closure by lack of patronage. Through skill and judgment of licensees, however, some country pubs have managed to retain their charm while responding to the market for food and family entertainment. Hats off to those publicans who cherish their pubs and serve their local communities. They receive little thanks for the business risk they take and long hours they put in every week. Most of all, thanks go to those who have the good sense to keep some areas of their pub traditional rather than giving it over entirely to a commercialism which invades most of our lives. This is what is now commonly described as post-modern society!

Therefore, our position is clear. The country pub usually survives by selling both food and drink, so publicans do not normally welcome people who bring their own sandwiches. Nor do they like muddy boots, for few have flag floors these days. What they do like is to see people enjoying the great outdoors and then relaxing in their pub whether for a drink or food, or both!

The subject of families and pubs tends to be more controversial. The law states that children should not be at the bar – end of story.

Please respect this and remember that some pubs are simply not geared up for children. Other places welcome families and provide facilities accordingly. Try these as you will be happier, so will your children and those who have invested in facilities will be repaid.

Opening times are given for guidance only. If the weather is warm and a pub is busy, the lunchtime hours are more likely to be extended in most pubs. Sunday times are not included unless a publican has mentioned specifically that the pub is open all day. Most stay open from noon until 3pm and re-open at 7pm in the evening.

The Breweries

Wherever possible, we have chosen pubs where the beer is known to be good and where there is a choice. The brewing industry in this country is moving in the direction of many other North European states. Soon, there will be two or three breweries which dominate the entire business. Their products will be available everywhere and choice will be limited as few competitors will be able to penetrate their outlets. Staffordshire is the epicentre of the entire process, for the brewing capital of England is undisputedly Burton-upon-Trent. This is where Bass and Carlsberg-Tetley have their headquarters, almost side by side.

Bass is one of the oldest breweries in the country and many love its premium beer, Draught Bass. Carlsberg-Tetley is the arch-rival and trades under several names, including brew pubs such as Firkin. Bass is currently (1997) attempting to merge with Carlsberg-Tetley, and this will make Bass Britain's biggest brewer.

Not all is lost, however, for in recent years Staffordshire has become home to a number of smaller breweries. They are known for their distinctive brews and many of us would love to drink their brews if only they were more widely available. There is little chance of that, however, for their major problem is to find outlets, most of which are currently tied to the big brewers. Anyone who has tasted the beers from Burton Bridge, Enville, or Titanic will know that they brew classic beers. They are tasty to drink and cost no more than those on offer from the giants. In contrast, in our opinion, beers from the big breweries tend to be far blander.

That's why we hope our readers will seek out the beers from the following breweries. It is not that easy as there are very few genuine free houses. **The Tap and Spile** in Stafford stocks unusual brews from small breweries as do a limited number of free houses where the landlord has a genuine choice. For example, **The Village Tavern**

The Burton Bridge Brewery Tap at Burton upon Trent

in Outwoods and **The Fox** at Marston offer a range from small breweries.

To help you in your search for real Staffordshire brews here's a run down of the nearby small independent breweries which serve the area:

Burton Bridge (Burton upon Trent)

The little brewery in Bridge Street has been brewing with gusto since 1982 and now supplies free houses in the region. There is a wide range of brews from XL and Bridge Bitter to Old Expensive, a rather powerful Christmas ale which you will not forget in a hurry. Fortunately, there is a brewery tap, The Burton Bridge Inn, which is well worth the pilgrimage.

Eccleshall

The Eccleshall Brewery was established in 1995 producing a range of beers named 'Slaters Ales' after the owners. It is rapidly gaining a reputation locally as a good pint. Try the Original for a hoppy brew. The brewery tap is the George Hotel in Eccleshall which is located by the bus stop for Stafford, which is rather fortunate.

Enville

The Enville brewery is another success story. The new brewery uses the water source once used by an earlier village brewery. The latter closed in 1919 but Enville is back with vengeance. The brewery uses honey from local beehives and, whilst strictly top secret, many of the recipes have been passed down from the brewer's great-great aunt. In one of the authors' favourite local it is always the fastest selling beer on the guest range.

Lichfield

Started by CAMRA members in 1992, this enterprising brewery produces a range of inspiring brews. It loves to devise commemorative brews for all manner of occasions and has a strong local following. It is available in several of the city's free houses and hopefully at the Swan with Two Necks at Longdon when you call.

The Rising Sun (Shraley Brook)

Brewing since 1989, the range of beers include Rising, Setting and Sunstroke! It sells mainly into the free trade in North Staffordshire, so is hard to come by in South Staffs. You could always take a trip north to The Rising Sun pub at Shraley Brook, which is the brewery tap.

Titanic Burslem)

Titanic ales are rather special, for they arrived in Stoke-on-Trent when things were looking sad on the beer scene. The brewery and its brews are themed after the ill-fated Titanic ocean liner, or more accurately to honour the last man on the bridge, Captain Smith.

Fortunately, those who live in the south of the county no longer have to journey to Burslem for the nectar, but can call into the Stafford Arms Hotel in Stafford, where they will find the beer in tip-top condition.

Batham (Delph)

Established in 1877, this family brewery is a legend in the Black Country and a visit to the Bull and Bladder at Delph is virtually compulsory for anyone who enjoys a beer. Try the mild as well as the bitter for they both tantalise the taste buds.

Holden's (Woodsetton)

In this book, you will also come across at least one of Holden's pubs, The Bell at Trysull. The brewery was established at Woodsetton in 1916 and now flourishes throughout the Black Country. The mild, bitter and other brews are fine ales.

You might also find brews from the following Shropshire breweries who seek outlets in Staffordshire.

Hanby (Wem)

Hanby Ales was established in 1988 after Greenall's closed the town's brewery. It has grown ever since and the brews are available in an increasing number of Shropshire free houses but also in Staffordshire. The Drawell bitter is exceptionally pleasant and if all else fails you will find that the landlord has plenty on tap for you at the brewery's tied house, The Star, in Market Drayton.

Salopian (Shrewsbury)

Salopian is a recent arrival on the scene which brews a range of beers in Shrewsbury. It aims to penetrate the guest beer market. This is a very welcome addition.

Whim (Hartington)

Another recent addition is Whim Ales from Hartington which is served at the brewery's pub in Leek, The Wilkes Head.

Wood (Wistanstow)

Founded by the Wood family in 1980 the brewery supplies a great range of beers to free houses. The brewery tap is The Plough at Wistanstow near Craven Arms.

Large regional breweries which feature in the county are Banks's of Wolverhampton and Marston's from Burton upon Trent, both of which have a number of houses in the area and both of which enjoy a good reputation with the drinker.

Join the Club!

If you enjoy walking, then the best thing you can do to help safeguard footpaths is to join the Ramblers' Association 1/5 Wandsworth Road, London, SW8 2XX. Tel 0171 582 6878

If you want choice in beers and pubs, then join the Campaign For Real Ale, 230 Hatfield Road, St Albans, Herts, AL1 4LW. Tel 01727 867201.

1. Abbots Bromley

Route: Abbots Bromley – Radmore Fields Farm – Beacon Bank – Abbots Bromley

Distance: 3 miles (5km)

Map: OS Pathfinder 851 Abbots Bromley

Start: The Crown, opposite the Butter Cross

Access: Unfortunately, there is only a limited bus service to Abbots Bromley from Burton, Stafford and Uttoxeter. It is the meeting point of a number of roads, the B5013 from Uttoxeter, and Rugeley, the B5243 from Burton-upon-Trent. There is limited car parking along School Lane.

The Royal Oak. 01283 840117

There are five pubs remaining in Abbots Bromley, all of which are on the High Street. Without exception they have in recent years aimed for the food market yet most maintain a balance between offering a locals' bar or area as well as developing areas for eating. The Royal Oak welcomes walkers. Its usual opening times are 12pm – 2.30pm and 6.30pm onwards on Mondays to Saturdays. It serves food in the bar but the pub also has a restaurant. Families are welcome and there is a small garden which is great for summertime drinking. On handpull is Marstons Pedigree and there is a frequently-changing guest beer. The authors also recommend The Crown, opposite the Butter Cross, as a pleasant place to call as it still retains a separate and often lively bar to the lounge.

Abbots Bromley

Abbots Bromley must be one of the prettiest of Staffordshire villages. It is justly famous for its annual Horn Dance, performed around the village and the parish in early September, an all-day event which involves treading many paths and calling at numerous places of

The Butter Cross, Abbots Bromley

refreshment. The performers of the ritual need real stamina to cope with both the mileage involved and the number of stops for refreshment! Six men usually set out dressed with mock reindeer heads and real antlers followed by others depicting the likes of Maid Marian, Robin Hood, a Jester and Hobby Horse – rich mythical characters of previous centuries. The horns are then returned to the 13th century parish church until the following year. The ancient Butter Cross, with its slate roof supported by substantial timber pillars stands in the centre of village and is probably the best known landmark in the area. Some say that the inveterate traveller Samuel Johnson used to rest awhile here on his way to Uttoxeter. It is more likely than the tale that Dick Turpin stayed at The Goat's Head after buying a horse at Rugeley fair. Nearby are several other interesting buildings such as Church House, a half-timbered building dating from the early 17th century and Hall Hill Manor Farm, reputedly where Mary Queen of Scots rested on her way to Tutbury Castle.

The Walk

1. Start from the entrance to The Crown Inn opposite the Butter Cross. Turn right to walk up School Road soon to pass the school. Turn next right into Swan Lane, to walk by houses to the end of the cul-de-sac. Go right at end and then first left, (i.e. do not enter the cricket ground.)

2. Cross a stile into a field and continue slightly left. Go through a gap and head slightly left, down-field, to a footbridge across the Dunstal Brook, and ahead to a stile beneath tree. Climb up the field ahead to cross the next stile. Rise up the bank. You come to a stile on the left by the water trough. Go over this and then head to the right over the next stile. Continue ahead and cross a stile by the gate and walk up a track to the road at Radmore Wood, although there appears to be little left of any woodland here.

3. Go over the road and keep ahead to cross a stile by the gate and 100 metres along drive cross a stile on the left. Radmore Fields Farm stands to your right. Head right down the hillside pasture where you cross a stile in a thick hedge. Go right to walk down to the road

4. Turn left at the road. As you near the farmhouse at Moors look right for a stile before. There is a signpost here. Head slightly right across the large field, often planted with cereal, but the path is usually well-trodden to a stile. Follow hedge on the left, then cross a track. Continue ahead on a farm track which skirts to the right of buildings and ahead to a road.

5. Pass Beacon Bank farm which is to your left and after 30 paces or so, go right through a bridleway gate. Continue through a gateway and ahead along a gentle ridge above Abbots Bromley. This affords good views of the old township and beyond. Pass through another bridle gate. You then come to a corner where you will see a stile on the left by gate at a spot known as The Clump.

6. This is where you join a cross-path. Go right here, heading slightly left to a barred gate. Once through, continue ahead, now keeping company with the hedge to your right. As this bends

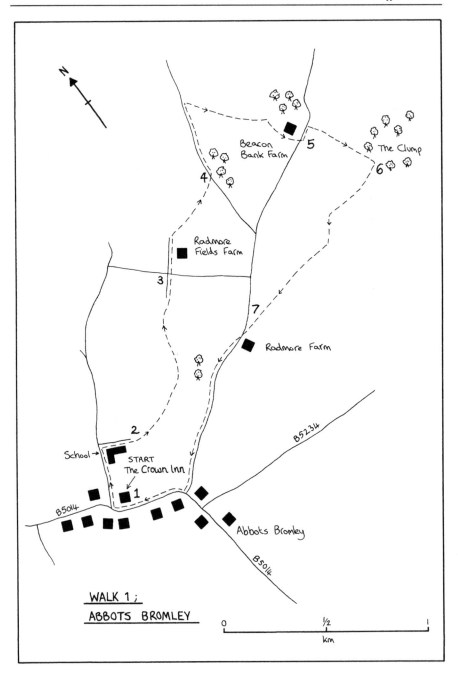

N

Beacon
Bank Farm

5

The Clump

4

6

Radmore
Fields Farm

3

7

Radmore Farm

B5234

2

School →

START
The Crown Inn

1

B5014

Abbots Bromley

B5014

WALK 1;
ABBOTS BROMLEY

0   ½   1
                    km

right, cut left (field corner opposite) and cross to a barred gate. Walk through it and head slightly left towards school buildings. Pass through hawthorns in a corner, then drop down bank to a stile. Head slightly left through a narrow enclosure to cross a foot bridge over the Ash Brook. Go left and climb a stile into the next field. Head slightly right towards Radmore Farm. Go over two stiles to join the road.

7. Turn left to wander along the quietest of lanes back into the village. At the main road go right to walk back to the Butter Cross.

2. Acton Trussell

Route: Acton Trussell – Bednall – Teddesley Park – Shutthill Bridge – Acton Trussell

Distance: 5 miles (8 km)

Map: OS Pathfinder 871 Cannock (North)

Start: The Moathouse public house

Access: There is a limited bus service to Acton Trussell but a more frequent one to Acton Gate on the A449. Travel on the A449 out of Stafford but look for a turning on the left at Acton Gate (i.e. before reaching the motorway interchange). This lane leads to Acton Trussell village where there is limited on-street parking near the church and in the village. Please park considerately.

The Moathouse. 01785 712217

The Moathouse, as its name suggests was originally a 15th century manor house and the scant remains of the moat earthworks can still be seen. Some suggest that in earlier times this was also the site of a Roman villa.

As an inn, it has become very popular over the years, not only building a reputation for good food but also for its beer. Usual opening hours are 11.00 – 3pm and 6.30pm – 11pm (10.30pm on Sundays). Bar and restaurant. Bar meals are served Monday to Friday 12pm – 2pm and 6.30pm – 9.30pm, also Saturday lunchtime. Families are welcome and there is a large garden. On handpull are Marston Pedigree, Banks's Mild plus two guest beers.

Acton Trussell

The dormitory village of Acton Trussell stands by the tranquil waters of the Staffordshire and Worcestershire canal, a quiet place disturbed only by the hum of the nearby M6 motorway.

The Moathouse, Acton Trussell

The parish church stands aloof from the village, a not-uncommon phenomenon where communities have developed centuries after the ecclesiastical base was established.

The Walk

1. From The Moat House entrance, turn left to walk through the village. At the next junction, bear right along Barn End Road and continue ahead at the triangular junction along Acton Hill. Turn right along a narrow lane signposted to Bednall.

2. This is a quiet road which comes to a staggered junction where you bear left and then almost immediately right. This is soon joined by another lane and you continue ahead towards the quiet hamlet of Bednall, where in contrast to Acton Trussell, houses nestle around the Victorian church.

3. Turn right here along a 'No Through Road' towards Teddesley where there are views to the left of Cannock Chase, not much

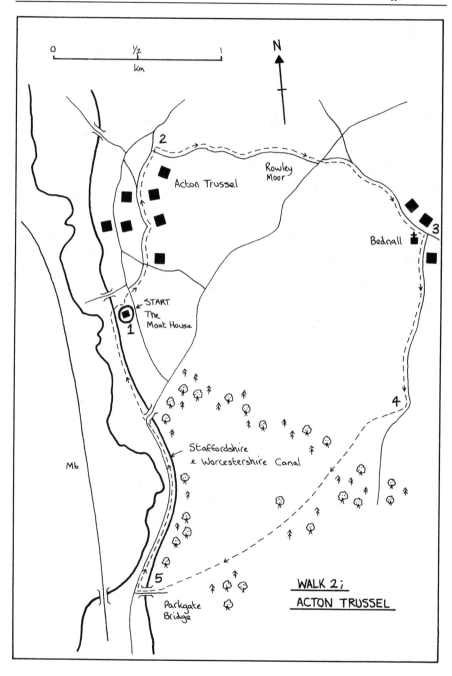

0   ½   1
km

N

2

Acton Trussel

Rowley
Moor

3
Bednall

START
The
Moat House
1

4

Staffordshire
& Worcestershire Canal

M6

5

Parkgate
Bridge

WALK 2;
ACTON TRUSSEL

more than a mile away. The lane passes between fields, then bears slightly right and left to approach a house.

4. Your way, however, is to the right, as signposted along the Staffordshire Way. At the end of the field go left over the stile by a gate and head slightly right across the pasture to enter woodland. Once through, keep ahead through the fields as signposted until you reach a stile in a field corner. Cross it and turn right to follow the boundary as far as a little bridge on the right. Go over this and again follow the field's edge to the tree belt and then left along the bottom until you reach a gate to the rear of a boatyard complex at Parkgate.

5. There is a stile by the gate leading on to a wider track over the Staffordshire and Worcestershire canal. Turn right to join the towpath and walk along it beneath Shutthill Bridge. Continue ahead until you reach the village and you can see across the canal to the Moathouse. Go right over the next bridge and right again to reach your goal.

3. Alrewas

Route: Alrewas – Bagnall Lock – Fradley Junction – Fradley – Alrewas

Distance: 5½ miles (9km)

Map: OS Pathfinder Map 872 Rugeley and Lichfield (North)

Start: George and Dragon, High Street, Alrewas

Access: Alrewas lies just off the main A38 road between Burton-upon-Trent and Lichfield.

The George and Dragon. 01283 791476

The George and Dragon is an impressive-looking pub which is well known for its community spirit in the town. Events organised by locals include a bike ride in April, and a triathlon in September. It has a large, open lounge bar which always has a cheerful atmosphere. Marston's Pedigree is on hand pump. Usual opening hours are 11pm – 2.30pm and 5pm – 11pm on Mondays to Saturdays. Bar meals are served 12.00 – 2pm and 7pm – 9.30pm. Families welcome. There is a Beer garden and play area to the rear.

Alrewas

Not far from Lichfield is Alrewas, a pleasant township exhibiting many fine buildings including centuries old thatch and half timbered houses. This is canal walking territory too so it seemed an obvious choice for inclusion in this book: a stroll along the Trent and Mersey to Fradley Junction and back by way of Fradley village. Fradley Junction is something of a mecca for canal enthusiasts as the carefully restored buildings here belong to the era of the narrow boat. Alrewas used to be known locally for basket making. Between the river and the canal there used to be osier beds, where special willows were cultivated. Many of the houses in the village belonged to estate workers, as the Earl of Lichfield used to own most of the

The Trent and Mersey Canal at Alrewas

land at one time. Eel fishery was a thriving trade here, too. It is primarily a dormitory town now, though there are many reminders of its past.

The Walk

1. From the George and Dragon public house in Alrewas, turn left and then at the war memorial go right to pass the post office and The Crown public house. Turn left into Church Road, go over the bridge and turn left to join the towpath. On the left are several characterful thatched and red brick cottages, on the right the impressive parish church. Pass near to the Navigation pub at Bridge 47.

2. Cross the road and walk by Bagnall Lock. The walk is easy. You simply follow the towpath for over half a mile up to Fradley Junction through low-lying arable farmland in the Vale of Trent.

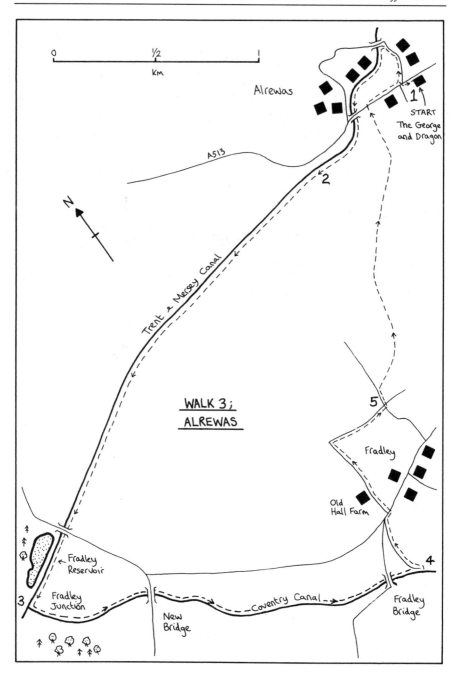

0   ½   1
km

Alrewas

A513

N

Trent & Mersey Canal

START
The George
and Dragon

1

2

WALK 3;
ALREWAS

5

Fradley

Old
Hall Farm

Fradley
Reservoir

Fradley
Junction

3

New
Bridge

Coventry Canal

4

Fradley
Bridge

3. Fradley Junction is an attractive place with 18th and 19th century dwellings and buildings nestled around the junction of the Trent and Mersey with the Coventry Canal. The colourful boats make it all the more interesting. Most will be tempted to stop for refreshment, as the handsome Swan public house stands temptingly on the right. Cross Junction Lock to pass Wharf House and follow the towpath of the Coventry Canal towards the village of Fradley. It is a good mile, and you know you are approaching as you walk beneath Fradley Bridge, Number 90.

4. Beyond the bridge is a row of cottages on the left. Go through the gate here. The track runs ahead past the cottages and then you bear right at a junction, through a white barred gate. At the next gate join an access road. This leads to a main road in Fradley village. Pass a school and a church then take the next left along Old Hall Lane which bends right to skirt houses.

5. At the cross roads, go left into Long Lane. After about 100 paces, beyond a cottage, go right and over a stile. Head across the field towards cottages. You should just be able to see the tower of Alrewas Church. Cross a stile onto a road. Opposite a house bear left over a stile by an electric telegraph pole. You go right to the field corner and then turn left to follow the field's edge, very often in crop with beet or brussels. Cut through a field corner and then go slightly right through the next field. Cross a stile and continue in a similar direction. Bear right for 50 paces and look for a stile on the right. Head slightly right.

6. Cross a road and another stile. Keep ahead across the edge of a playing field. The right of way is to the right of the club house. Go through the playing area to the main road. Turn right for the centre of Alrewas.

4. Bobbington

Route: Bobbington – Leaton – Mere Copse – Bobbington Mills – Bobbington

Distance: 3 miles (5km)

Map: OS Pathfinders 912 Wolverhampton, and Stourbridge 933

Start: The Red Lion, Bobbington

Access: There is a limited bus service on Monday to Saturdays from Wolverhampton which allows time for a walk and refreshment. Bobbington lies in the very south of the county and is best approached off the A449 then following signs for Highgate Common and Bobbington south of Wombourne. There is limited street parking in the village.

The Red Lion. 01384 221237

The Red Lion has been renovated in recent years, making it more open plan than before. It now has a large lounge and an equally large bar. Furthermore, there are extensive gardens and playground which make it a good family choice for the summertime, when there is sometimes a barbecue on the patio. On handpull are M&B mild, Bass and Theakstons brews. There are some interesting exhibits on the wall which unfold a little of the history of the pub. It was first recorded as an ale house in 1820, offering home-brewed cider, ale and porter. The two key property holders in the area, the Earl of Stanford of Enville Hall and William Mosley of Leadon Hall, allowed 18-hour opening. Mild was certainly the drink in those times. Nowadays the pub is very much involved in the community. In particular, it is home to an amateur boxing club which uses the old outbuildings. There are numerous charity events throughout the year. Usual opening times are 12pm – 3pm and 6.30pm – 11pm.

Bobbington church

Bobbington

Bobbington is steeped in antiquity. It was certainly mentioned in the Domesday Book and the small parish church is thought to be 11th century with parts remaining from an earlier Saxon building. Originally called St Mary's, it was re-dedicated to The Holy Cross in 1905. There is a wrought-iron flower stand to commemorate the death of HRH Prince William of Gloucester, killed in an air crash in 1972 at the nearby Halfpenny Green Airfield. Nearby stands historic Blakelands, a listed 17th century Queen Anne house with exquisite gardens, orchard and fish pool. Also nearby is Staffordshire's only vineyard – Halfpenny Green Vineyard, with visitor centre. Their wines have achieved several top awards in recent years.

The Walk

1. From the entrance to The Red Lion turn left and walk to the corner. Cross the road and follow a path which squeezes between gardens to a stile which exits in a field. Walk ahead along the hedge to cross another stile. Then continue directly ahead along a narrow strip between crops.

2. At the far end, go left through a gateway and then turn right on the track before Leaton Cottages. Go next left through a gap into a field, with a hedge on your right. Go through a gap in the next boundary and keep ahead. You reach a corner where the hedge bears right. You do not. Instead head slightly left across the remainder of the field to the far left corner.

3. Do not go through the gate but turn right to walk up the field with a hedge now on your left which leads into a narrow belt of woodland. Cross the stile and walk ahead. The terrain is flat and the soil is rich, so there is a different crop in almost every field. Go through another gap where a stile once stood. Keep as close to the hedge as possible and come to a wood, Mere Copse and something of a relief after all of that arable farming.

4. Cross a stile by the wood and walk on through a pasture to a gateway and then go left to re join the field edge on the left towards Salter's Park Farm. Cross the stile to the left of the farm

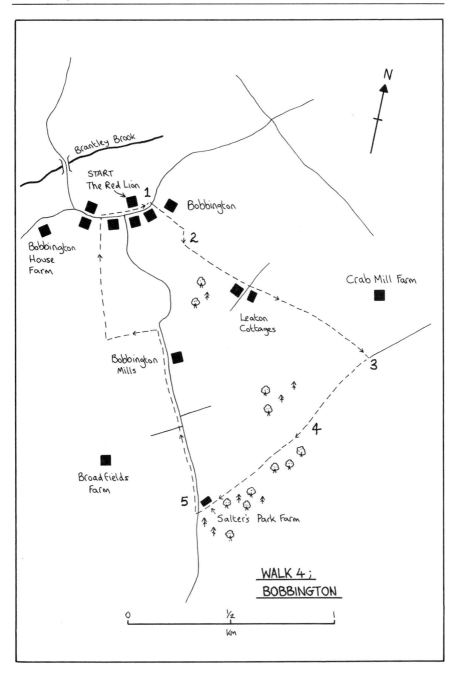

WALK 4;
BOBBINGTON

buildings and a sleeper footbridge before proceeding along the fence by the farm. Exit onto the road by way of a stile.

5. Turn right and walk towards Bobbington for less than half a mile until you see an agricultural store on the right. At the corner of the road, go left over a stile and follow the field's edge on the left along the field, one which is often in cereal crop. Look for the meeting of a cross path coming in at a gate on the left. Go right here across the field on a well-worn path. This crosses a farm track and continues through a gateway and ahead. The path then leads between gardens to the main road in Bobbington. Turn right for the Red Lion.

5. Brewood

Route: Brewood – Dean's Hall Bridge – Chillington Avenue – Giffard's Cross – Shropshire Union Canal – Brewood

Distance: 4 miles (6km)

Map: OS Pathfinder 891 Wolverhampton (North)

Start: The Lion, Brewood

Access: Brewood is served by a bus service from Wolverhampton, daily including Sundays. Travel on the A449 from Stafford or Wolverhampton and turn at Coven for Brewood. There is a car park in the village.

The Swan. 01902 850330

Brewood is fortunate in having a number of good hostelries, two of which stand opposite each other in the Market Square. With a Good Beer Guide entry in 1996, The Swan serves a beer on handpull from the Scottish and Newcastle range as well as Draught Bass and, a guest beer. Usual opening times: 11pm – 3pm with meals served until 2pm. It re-opens at 7pm. There is a lounge bar and, unusually, a skittle alley upstairs. In case your walk builds a thirst we can advise you that there are a number of pubs in the village including the three mentioned below. Opposite The Swan is The Lion which is open at lunch and early evening and often all day in summer. Banks' Mild and Draught Bass are available. Also in Brewood is the Admiral Rodney, just down from the church and good for families as the garden is very pleasant. The Bridge by the canal, is also a welcoming pub. In short, there is a pub in every direction in Brewood.

Brewood

It is always a pleasure to call in to the handsome village of Brewood in South Staffordshire. Local residents and the Civic Society in particular take a real pride in their community – and it shows. Always of interest is the Georgian Speedwell Castle, named after the horse on which the owner waged sufficient funds to win a fortune. He went on then to build the house! The streets which radiate from Brewood's impressive church are full of attractive historic houses. The village dates from Roman times when fort was built to defend nearby Watling Street. Many places nearby are connected with the flight of Charles II after the Battle of Worcester in 1651. These include Boscobel House where Charles took refuge in an oak tree (which later gave its name to the many Royal Oak pubs in the area). Chillington Hall can be seen on the ramble, a fine dwelling which was once the home of the Giffard family. Built on the site of an earlier castle it looks so impressive down the Avenue. It is open to the public on certain days in the summer.

The Walk

1. Start the ramble from the Swan Public house and turn right to walk along Church Road and past the church. The road bends left and you go right along a ginnel between cottages to a track. Turn left and then go right over a stile to enter a field.

2. Head slightly left down the field, cross a stile and walk up to Dean's Hall bridge over the Shropshire Union canal, one of the loveliest navigations in the country. It has always been used for recreational purposes in and around Brewood during this century. Go right over the bridge and along a track. This bends left at a junction and then right to pass by the garden of Woolley Farm.

3. The track soon curves right and begins to descend but you keep ahead as waymarked on the Staffordshire Way. Go through a meadow to eventually cross stiles and The Avenue, with its fine view of Chillington Hall.

4. The path exits onto a road. Go left and follow this to a junction with a main road. Turn left and see Giffard's Cross in the cottage garden. This is a reminder of the gallant 16th-century deed of Sir John Giffard who killed a panther which had escaped from its cage.

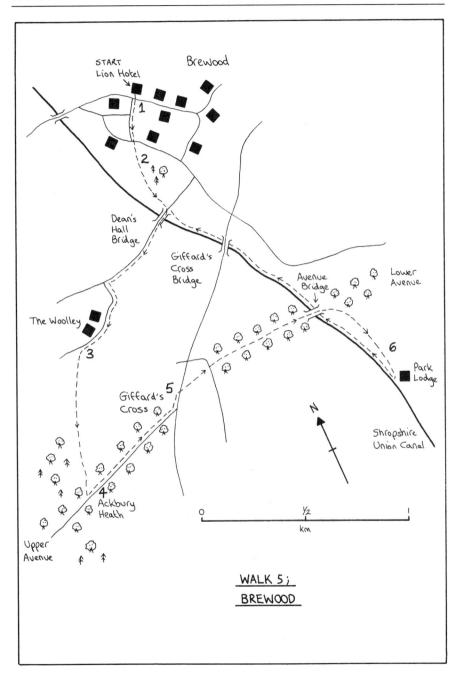

START
Lion Hotel
Brewood

1

2

Dean's
Hall
Bridge

Giffard's
Cross
Bridge

Avenue
Bridge

Lower
Avenue

The Woolley

3

6

Park
Lodge

Giffard's 5
Cross

N

Shropshire
Union Canal

4
Ackbury
Heath

Upper
Avenue

0   ½   1
km

WALK 5;
BREWOOD

5. Cross the main road with care and enter a path, through a gate, and ahead along a wooded section of the Avenue. Cross another road and go through a gate to walk ahead again. The path runs across a splendidly ornate bridge over the Shropshire Union Canal. Bear slightly right here along a lesser path through trees. Cross the stile to enter a field and follow the field's edge on the right to the next field corner, ignoring the bridge on the right. Cross a stile and keep ahead. You can see a building just to the left.

6. Your way is over a stile on the right to gain access to the towpath of the Shropshire Union opposite a small wharf. Go right along the towpath, through the cutting and under the ornate bridge. At the second bridge after this, exit up the bank. This is where you began your outward stroll. Retrace your steps back across two fields to Brewood, aiming for the church spire. Alternatively, you can continue if you wish, along the canal to the next bridge, where you rise up by the Bridge Inn. Go left for the Market Square.

The magnificent spire of Brewood Church

6. Chorley

Route: Chorley – Gentleshaw Moor – Creswell Green – Chorley

Distance: 4 miles (6 km)

Map: OS Pathfinder 872 Rugeley and Lichfield

Start: The Malt Shovel, Chorley

Access: Chorley has an infrequent service. Contact Staffordshire Bus on (01785) 223344. Travel on the A51 towards Lichfield turning right at Longdon (towards Gentleshaw) or at Longdon Green for Farewell and Chorley. There is limited parking in the village.

The Malt Shovel. 01543 685277

The Malt Shovel is a traditional village pub standing alongside the green. It has a lounge and bar of character. The Malt Shovel is open every day from 12.00 – 3pm and 7pm – 11pm. No food is served. Unfortunately children are not accommodated inside but there is a garden for summer months. Ansells Bitter, Mild and Tetley Bitter plus a guest beer are usually available on hand pull. It is a popular spot with visitors and features highly in village life.

Chorley

According to local people this sleepy village on the edge of Cannock Chase has been known to re-direct many a delivery van in search of its namesake in Lancashire. It is an easy enough mistake to make but a costly one, for the two are a good hundred miles apart. The Staffordshire Chorley retains a strong farming community but as with many rural communities more villagers are now retired or work in nearby towns. One of a number of interesting farmsteads is Lodge Farm which dates from 1737.

The Malt Shovel, Chorley

The Walk

1. Begin the ramble from the front entrance of the Malt Shovel public house in Chorley. Turn left along Lodge Lane. At the T-junction go left again but at the next junction take the right fork. This narrow thoroughfare rises to a junction where there is a view of a windmill at Windmill Bank. Cross over to enter a bridleway which winds its way down to the Maple Brook, a babbling stream which has to be forded, so expect to get your feet wet.

2. The track rises to a junction bordered by brambles where you keep left and continue to climb the bank under tree cover. It exits onto a road and a complete change of scenery, open moorland stretching to Gentleshaw Hill. It is a real change of scenery. Go over the road and join a green track. Turn left and walk down the hillside almost parallel to the road. This runs down to the right of a crossroads.

3. Go over the road and cross two stiles by gates in succession.

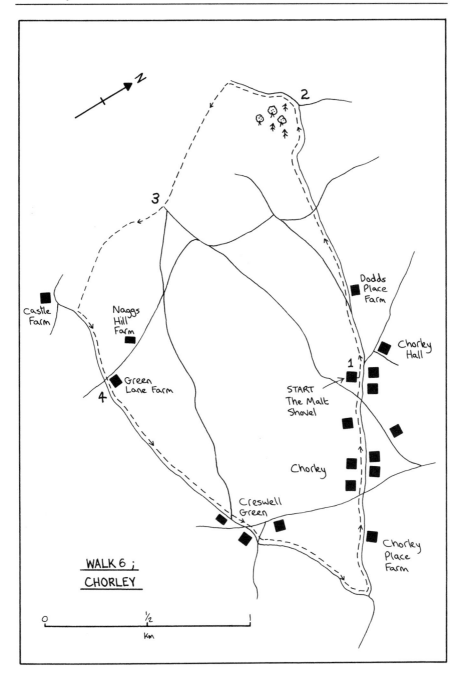

WALK 6 ;
CHORLEY

Continue down the hillside to cross another stile. The path curves left to yet another stile. Once over, head slightly right to cross a bridge over a trickle of a stream. Then go left, walking with a hedge on your left to a barred gate. Once on the road bear left to walk past The Drill Inn and climb to a crossroads.

4. Cross over and follow this delightful bridleway which happens to be a section of the long distance route, the Heart of England Way. Join a lane to enter the hamlet of Creswell Green nestled around the Nelson Arms which you happen to pass by. Go right at the T-junction and where the two roads meet, turn left to go through a stream and wood. Cross a stile and then follow the water meadows ahead crossing three stiles before reaching a road. Turn left for Chorley, rising steadily to the village. Ignore turns to the left and right and return to the Malt Shovel, no doubt in need of refreshment after that last climb.

7. Church Eaton

Route: Church Eaton – Shropshire Union Canal – High Onn Bridge – Church Eaton Green – Church Eaton

Distance: 4 miles (6 km)

Map: OS Pathfinder 871 Cannock (North)

Start: Royal Oak, Church Eaton

Access: Travel to Penkridge and turn right onto the Brewood Road, then right again at Cuttlestone Bridge. Alternatively, travel on the A518 road out of Stafford to Haughton and bear left in the village. There is limited on-street parking In Church Eaton.

The Royal Oak. 01785 823078

The Royal Oak is said to have been named after the tree standing in the car park which is thought to have been seeded from the 'King Charles' oak tree (see Walk 5). The pub in recent years has been modernised and offers one large room which is split between a bar and restaurant area. It is open evenings only from 6.30pm weekdays, and Saturday & Sunday lunchtimes. Bar and restaurant meals are available and families are welcome. There are seats outside and a beer garden. On handpull are Wadworth 6x, Draught Bass, Boddingtons and other selected guest beers.

Church Eaton

The quiet village of Church Eaton lies to the south-west of Stafford and no more than a mile from an idyllic stretch of the Shropshire Union Canal, a firm favourite of ramblers in this area. The oldest quarter of the village is around its church which has both a tower and spire. Close to the church is the Victorian village institute and also the rectory. Until recently the village was entirely engaged in

The Trent and Mersey Canal near Church Eaton

agriculture but now it is mainly a dormitory community for Stafford. Farms, however, can still be found in and around the village.

The Walk

1. Start from the Royal Oak public house, at the opposite end of the village to the attractive parish church. It must be one of the best-kept churchyards in the area with daffodils in Spring, tulips and wallflowers as well as roses pruned to perfection. Nearby is the old village water pump and kissing gate. From the Royal Oak, turn left along Wood Eaton Road. Follow this for approximately one quarter of a mile where you pass by the few cottages and farms which make up this settlement. The handsome Brookhouse Farm is to your left; just around the bend, look for a footpath on the left, signposted to Goosemoor. The path heads right by the barn and crosses a stile which leads onto a green track.

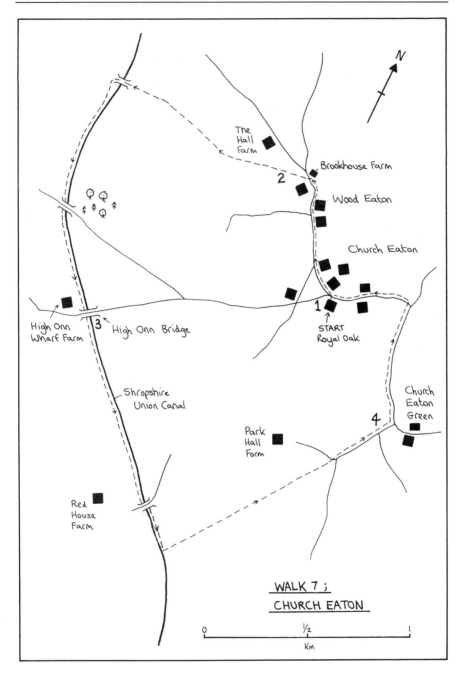

WALK 7 ;
CHURCH EATON

2. This soon finishes at a stile which brings you to a large pasture. Head slightly right towards a gate mid-field (rather than the gate on the left). Go through it and continue ahead in the next field. Cross a bridge and go left down to the towpath of the Shropshire Union Canal where you will see several leisure boats plying the water at this time of year. Pass beneath a bridge and cross sides at a roving bridge before reaching a small wharf at Higher Onn Bridge, a visual reminder that the canal was once a major carrier of agricultural produce.

3. Continue ahead to walk along a straight section of canal for about half a mile to the next bridge. Rise up to the road and cross over directly. Continue ahead above the canal but, after the length of a field, go left as signposted. Keep ahead along what was an old track and is now a bridleway. Go through the bridlegate and ahead to the next gate. Go through it to enter an old track which soon joins another by a cottage. The lane runs down slightly right to a road.

4. Turn left and follow this back into the village (ignoring turns to the right) passing the cricket pitch and village hall. Bear left at the church.

8. Colton

Route: Colton – Martlin-Hill – Stockwell Heath – Colton

Distance: 2½ miles (4 km)

Map: OS Pathfinder 851 Abbots Bromley

Start: The Greyhound

Access: Colton enjoys a bus service from Stafford on Mondays to Saturdays. By car it is best to travel to Rugeley then on the B5013, turning off for Colton as signposted

The Greyhound. 01889 586769

The Greyhound is a comfortable pub with a bar and lounge. Walkers are given a friendly welcome. It looks a very traditional pub from the outside with wooden bay windows. There is also a beer garden with tables outside. Families are welcome too. Usual opening hours are noon until 2.30pm and from 7pm although it is closed on Monday and Tuesday lunch in winter. Bar meals served 12pm – 2pm and 7pm – 9pm. The beer is invariably in excellent condition, Bank's Mild and Bitter.

Colton

East of Stafford is the historic village of Colton entered by the Brook Bridge where four large boulders can be seen, relics of an Ice Age deposited hereabouts. To the right, across a green, stands the parish church. The church was heavily restored in the last century replacing previous buildings. There are also several interesting houses in the village including the Queen Anne style Colton House. At Wolseley Bridge there is a restored 17th century thrashing barn, brought from Parchfields Farm, which has now become a craft centre, worth a visit. Also nearby is Belamour Hall was built in 1635 by Herbert Aston

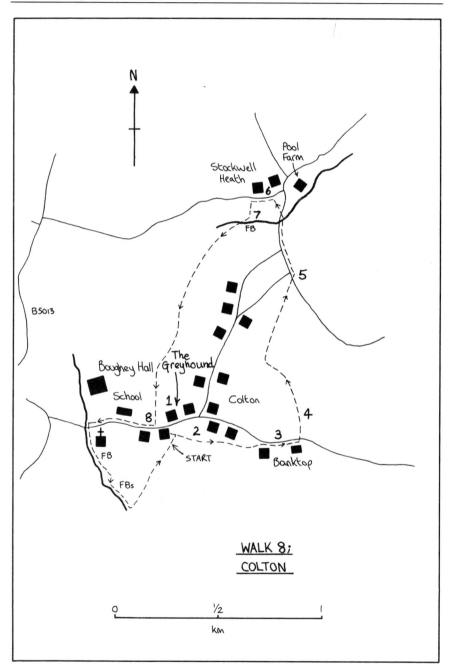

N

Pool
Farm

Stockwell
Heath

6

7
FB

5

The
Greyhound

Boughey Hall

School

Colton

1

8

4

START

2

3

Banktop

FB

FBs

B5013

WALK 8:
COLTON

0   ½   1
km

The Walk

1. This easy walk begins at The Greyhound. Go right to walk through the village towards the stream and bridge. Just before, turn left towards a stile by the brook and then ahead along a well-worn path. Cross a footbridge and continue through a small enclosure to another bridge. Once over go left and at the field corner bear left again, crossing a bridge and continuing to the houses beyond a Water Works.

2. Walk along the track to the road junction and turn right along Martlin Lane to pass this fine terrace. Cross a stile and at the electricity pole bear left to another stile. Climb the bank and continue ahead along the brow of the hill to a stile. Go over this and turn left. At the corner you come to a gate. Go through it and join the road by a house.

3. Turn right to descend a slope. Look for a memorial plaque on a gate on the left to a former resident who loved the countryside. Not far beyond go left along a path through brambles and scrub.

The Brook Bridge at Colton

This is not signposted nor clear, so be vigilant. If you come to the house on the right you have passed it!

4. The path leads into a field. Keep ahead along the hedge to a stile in the top corner. In the next field head for the outbuildings. Your way is through the gap to the right of the nearest building. The path is shown on the map as crossing the field, slightly left, to the bottom left corner although it is not evident on the ground. At this corner drop down through a gap on to the road.

5. Turn left to walk ahead to Stockwell Heath, a short section of road walking. Ignore turns to the left. Just after the bridge over the stream you can cut left and then right through a small enclosure to a road.

6. Turn left along Moor Lane, and just a round the corner beyond cottages, go left again to enter a field on the Staffordshire Way. A clear path leads down to a footbridge over the stream.

7. Go right up to a stile and then through a small enclosure to another. Your way is now approximately ahead as waymarked through a succession of fields. You are then guided right down to a stile set in fencing and once over keep left for 30 metres or so to a gate. Go through a narrow strip to and then through a field to the rear of the village hall.

8. The path joins a track onto the main village street. Go left to walk by the handsome Georgian dwellings to the Greyhound pub.

9. Enville

Route: Enville – Enville Hall – The Sheepwalks – Gilbert's Cross – Enville

Distance: 5 miles (8 km)

Map: OS Pathfinder 933 Stourbridge

Start: The Cat, Enville

Access: There is a limited bus service from Wolverhampton. Travel on the A458 road to Enville. There is limited parking near to the pub.

The Cat. 01384 872209

The Cat is a 16th century coaching Inn. There have been sightings of ghosts walking through the kitchens and footsteps are heard across the landing. There are several four-beamed rooms where you will find real fires in winter months. Usual opening times are Monday to Saturday 12pm – 3pm and 7pm – 11pm. Meals served at lunchtime, 12pm – 2pm and evenings from 7pm – 11pm. Please note that it is closed on Sundays due to a clause written into the covenant. Families are welcome; there is a beer garden with French boules. The pub serves mainly ales from the nearby Enville brewery which is associated with the Cat. These include Enville White and Gothic ale, but other guest beers are sold. There is a one-bedroomed fully furnished flat which can be used for bed and breakfast and will comfortably sleep four for those wishing to stay in the area.

Enville

The church of St Mary has an imposing tower, which is said to be reminiscent of Gloucester Cathedral. It is Norman in origin, but was much restored by famous church architect Gilbert Scott in the 1870s. The church stands on high ground above the village which contains several estate buildings from the 19th century. The 18th century Enville Hall set in landscaped parkland was created by the

Grey Family, the Earls of Stamford. On the edge of the estate is
Brindley Hall, at one time the home of James Brindley, the talented
canal builder from Derbyshire.

Enville Hall

The Walk

1. From the entrance to The Cat, turn right and right again to walk into the Enville Estate. Pass by the grand Stable Block but do not go through the white gates and along the track. Instead choose the stile to the right. Walk ahead through the field to cross a stile which leads into a small wood with a pool to the right. Home Farm is to the left.

2. Cross the stile and pass through a small enclosure to another stile. Now head slightly right up a large field. Catch a glimpse of the hall across the reflection of the pool; it is splendid scene. You will also note the monument to your left, one of several in this parkland. Join a track to rise up to a gateway. Go through it, then continue to climb the bank to a pair of gates. Choose the left hand one and bear slightly left again. Pause awhile to gain your breath and look back at Kinver Edge and the Kinver Church.

3. Keep ahead between woods and as you climb the shoulder you will see a farm. Strike right to join another footpath coming in from the left up from the farm to the gateway seen on your right. Cross the stile by it and now walk slightly right up the bank to meet the wood's edge. The view across South Staffordshire and Shropshire makes the effort worth it. You can also see the Malvern Hills from here. You reach a corner of the fencing. Bear slightly right (as waymarked) across the pasture and with a ruin of a house to the left. Go down the bank towards a wooded stream, bearing slightly left as waymarked.

4. Cross the stream and a stile. Then turn right and left along a field's edge. This climbs to a corner and a track. Go left beneath the branches of a large oak. Go right here between two posts and turn right to follow the field's edge. At the corner the path dips down to the right as waymarked. It bends left to a stile leading into a field. Cross the path which cuts directly across the crop to a gully and hedge. Cross the boundary here and follow the hedge on your left, up the field, to exit onto a road opposite a cottage.

5. Turn right and walk along the road to a cross-roads. Cross over and walk ahead. Within a quarter of a mile look for the Staffordshire Way markers on the right as you cross a stile into a field.

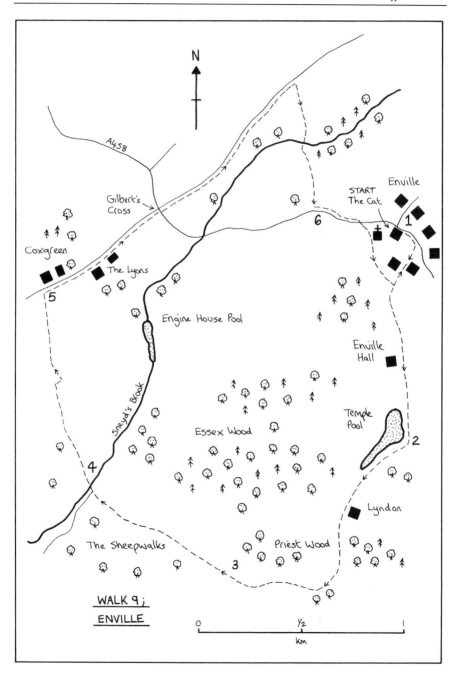

N

A458

Gilbert's
Cross

Coxgreen

The Lyons

5

Engine House Pool

Enville

START
The Cat

6

1

Enville
Hall

Sneyd's Brook

Essex Wood

Temple
Pool

2

4

Lyndon

The Sheepwalks

Priest Wood

3

WALK 9;
ENVILLE

0   ½   1
km

This county path is well walked and is clear on the ground. Follow it down to the field corner. The path dips down to a bridge and then ahead to a fence. Go left to cross the stiles and up a green lane. This brings you to a white gate. Go through it and bear slightly right along fencing to exit by the drive onto the main road.

6. Go left along the verge but choose carefully where you cross. Enter the churchyard car park and look at the clock faces to see whether the times agree. A path leads down through the gravestones to cross a stile into a field. Head slightly left across the field to a stile by a gate. Walk between gardens to the road and turn left to retrace your steps.

10. Gnosall

Route: Gnosall – Brough Hall – Audmore – Gnosall

Distance: 2½ miles (4km)

Map: OS Pathfinder 850 Stafford

Start: The Horns, Gnosall

Access: Gnosall is served by bus from Stafford on Mondays to Saturdays. Travel on the A518 from Stafford. There is limited car parking in the village

The Horns. 01785 822441

The Horns is a very friendly pub on the High Street with live entertainment every other Wednesday. Annual events include the June carnival and a Harvest Festival where the locals bring home-produced goods which are auctioned in the lounge and the money raised is split between local causes. Usual opening times: Monday to Friday, 11.30pm – 3pm and 6pm – 11pm; Saturday, 11.30pm – 11pm; Sunday, 11.30pm – 3pm and 7pm – 10.30pm. No food is available. The pub welcomes families and dogs! No garden, but there are tables and chairs on the car park. Bank's Mild, Bass, Worthington, and Highgate Mild are available on handpull.

Gnosall

The village was listed in the Domesday Book as Geneshall. The impressive Church of St Lawrence dates from 1080, and is a good one of the best examples in the county of a collegiate church. The Dukes Head (no longer a hostelry) near to the Horns has an Elizabethan facade, but parts probably date from earlier period. Nearby there is also the old lock-up, moved from its original site to make way for road improvements, and no longer acting as a deterrent for loutish behaviour. Both the Shropshire Union Canal and the railway stimulated trade in the area including a cement business for which

Gnosall church

Gnosall was once famous. The canal is a superb leisure resource, and the railway on which the last passenger train ran in 1964, is destined to become part of the National Cycle Network master-minded by engineering charity Sustrans.

The Walk

1. From the Horns, turn left towards Gnosall Post Office and gift shop. Walk along Audmore Road but soon turn left along Knightley Road. The road rises up and then drops down to a house by a junction. Go right to cross a stile and once over go right up the field.

2. Keep ahead, but cut right before the corner of field, over a stile. Follow the hedge in the left to cross a stile by a gateway. Go left and walk towards a bungalow, but cut right through the under-growth to a footbridge and stile.

3. Go left and cross a stile at the next building. Keep ahead to the next field boundary, cut left through a gateway and go ahead to the next one, hence avoiding the wire fence. Moor Lane Farm

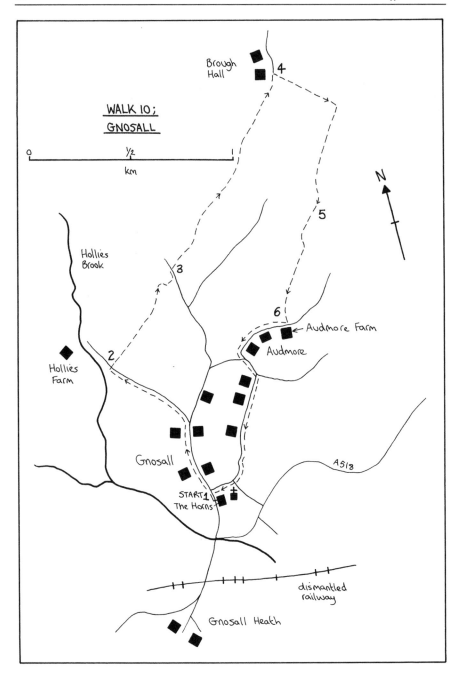

Brough
Hall

4

WALK 10;
GNOSALL

0   ½   1
              km

N

Hollies
Brook

3

5

6

Audmore Farm

Audmore

Hollies
Farm

2

Gnosall

A518

START 1
The Horns

dismantled
railway

Gnosall Heath

stands to the left. You come to a barred gate. Go through it and continue ahead. There is a pool to the left. Head towards the field corner and go slightly right to pass beneath an oak tree. Walk ahead along field edge to a barred gate Brough Hall Farm.

4. Go right on the road but at the corner continue ahead over the stile by a gate into the pasture. Cross a stile on the right by a water trough. Walk ahead to the hedge. Just before the corner, cut across to go through a hedge to the left of a pool. Go over a stile here.

5. Head slightly right across the field (usually planted with a cereal crop) heading to the right of a wood. Cross the boundary beneath an oak and you can now see the church clearly ahead. Go through the field, aiming for the church as your landmark. Cross a double stile and walk ahead across the pasture to a farm.

6. Go right on the road and, at the triangular junction, bear left. At the next junction go right along a residential street. Cross the wide road into Glebe Lane and keep ahead. Go right at the junction by the church and then left through the gate into the churchyard of the Parish church of St Lawrence. Then walk back to The Horns.

Gnosall

```
┌─────────────────────────────────────────────────────────┐
│                                                           │
│                 11. Great Haywood                         │
│                                                           │
└─────────────────────────────────────────────────────────┘
```

Route: Great Haywood – Staffordshire & Worcestershire Canal – Milford Common – Shugborough Park – Great Haywood

Distance: 4 miles (6km)

Map: OS Pathfinder 850 Stafford

Start: Clifford Arms, Great Haywood

Access: There is a regular bus service from Stafford to Great Haywood, daily including Sundays. Travel on the A51 to Great Haywood or from Stafford on the Tixall Road. There is limited car parking in the village

The Clifford Arms. 01889 881321

The Clifford Arms, which stands on the site of an old coaching house, is a good local pub situated in the centre of the village. There is a lounge and a bar where Draught Bass, Worthington Bitter and a guest ale are on tap. Usual opening hours are Monday to Thursday 12pm – 4pm and 7pm – 11pm. Friday and Saturday 12pm – 4pm and Sunday 12pm – 4pm and 7pm – 10.30pm. Sunday lunches served 12pm – 3pm. Monday to Saturday lunches 12pm – 2pm. Every evening, meals are served 7pm – 9.30pm. Families welcome and there is an outdoor drinking area.

Great Haywood

This walk offers a variety of landscape, a touch of historical interest and an opportunity to sample exquisite parkland in the heart of the county. Great Haywood has the longest packhorse bridge in England across the River Trent which is at its prettiest here. It dates from 16th century, and has 14 of original 40 arches remaining. It was built by the first Earl of Essex to enable his horses to be driven to Cannock Chase. Great Haywood has many links with the Anson family who were the benefactors who funded the Shugborough Hall and the driven parkland surrounding it. Many of those dispossessed of their dwellings in the process resettled in the village. Great Haywood has just about every form of transport, from the Trent and Mersey Canal to the railway, so it is quite a busy place. Buses stop regularly if everything else passes you by.

Tixall Hall Lodge, overlooking the canal near Great Haywood

The Walk

1. Start the walk from The Clifford Arms. Turn right from the Clifford Arms entrance to walk between fine houses to the railway and Trent and Mersey Canal. Before the historic Essex bridge, go left through a gap in the wall to the towpath where you go left again. You soon reach the junction with the Staffordshire and Worcestershire Canal.

2. Go under the fine arched bridge and turn left to pass the Old Toll House Crafts shop. This is an unusual section of canal for there are wide pools which almost look like natural basins. Walk by

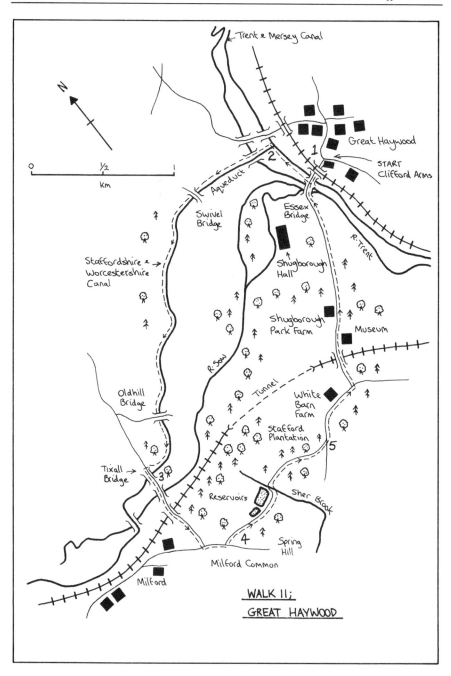

WALK II;
GREAT HAYWOOD

Tixall Locks at Old Hill Bridge, an attractive canal setting. Continue ahead to Tixall Bridge (Number 106).

3. Pass underneath then turn left up to the road. Walk ahead, facing the traffic, to cross the bridge over the River Sow and then to the main road by the entrance to Shugborough Hall. Walk up the left hand verge of the main road past a cautionary signpost to a small lay-by.

4. Go left here with an old wall on your left. Climb up to the underground reservoir tanks and head slightly right to cross other tracks and straight on down the hillside. Ignore the numerous tracks off to the left and right. Simply keep ahead until you reach an open green. A few paces on and you reach a main track. Go right down to the main road which is a bind but a necessary quarter of mile link to Shugborough Park

5. Turn left to walk along the verge, past another vehicle access point for Shugborough, by a bus stop and then opposite a house go left into the park along a shaded path. This joins a road. Keep ahead through the parkland, ignoring turns to the left and right. On the right is part of a 'Ha-Ha', a ditch and mound built to protect the view from Shugborough Hall. Then, you will pass the entrance to the working farm.

6. Pass the Tower of Winds on the left, one of the many follies throughout the Park which make it such a fascinating place. As the main drive bears left to Shugborough Hall go ahead along a narrow road which runs through to the Essex Bridge. There are great views of the hall on the way. Cross the bridge and return to Great Haywood where refreshment is available for thirsty walkers.

12. Hamstall Ridware

Route: Hamstall Ridware – Nethertown – Pipe Ridware – Hunger Hill – Hamstall Ridware

Distance: 3 miles (5 km)

Map: OS Pathfinder 872 Rugeley and Lichfield (North)

Start: The Shoulder of Mutton, Hamstall Ridware

Access: The Ridwares have a very limited bus service. By car, travel on the A51 to Rugeley, then the A513 and B5014. Turn right for Pipe Ridware and Hamstall Ridware. There is limited parking in the village so park considerately.

The Shoulder of Mutton.

This rare rural survivor stands in a group of houses near to the River Blithe. There is a welcoming front bar with a little nook where darts are played. Here you will find a very useful notice board which displays the works of a local historian advertising 'The Book – Hamstall Ridware', penned in 1988 at a price of £50. The Shoulder of Mutton is open lunchtimes except Mondays and from 7 pm in the evening. Lounge and restaurant area to rear. It serves Worthington Bitter on handpump as well as a guest beer.

Hamstall Ridware

Ridware means the folk of the river. As the four villages and hamlets of the same name – Hamstall, Hill, Mavesyn and Pipe Ridware – lie between the flowing waters of the Blithe and Trent, the name seems highly appropriate. Hamstall Ridware sits close to the Blithe, an attractive place with a church which is approached across a pasture and a handsome manor house nearby. This is the very epitome of rural England. Thus, it is barely surprising that Austen is said to have visited Hamstall rectory, one time home of her uncle, Edward Cooper.

Rugeley power station from the Ridwares

The Walk

1. Start the walk from The Shoulder of Mutton, Hamstall Ridware. Turn left and left again at the junction. At the edge of the village the road bends right. After Blythe House Farm you go left over a double stile. Follow the hedge on the left past barns into the flood plain of the River Blithe. Go through two gates and cross a stile by a hut. Then, go left and right to follow the field's edge.

2. Head slightly right across the field, aiming for the far right and indented corner. Go through a gateway and bear slightly right over the field to a stile by a gate. Farm buildings of Upper Netherton Farm, stand to the right.

3. Join a road, go left into a lost hamlet known as Nethertown. At a red brick dwelling known as Bancroft House, turn right along a track which soon bends left. You keep ahead along a bridleway. This can get wet and the growth is thick in places. It runs into a field. Follow the bridleway as best you can to the corner ahead, where there is a road.

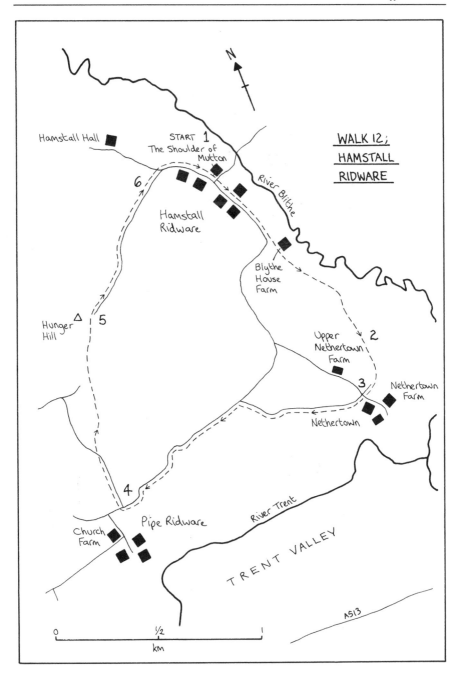

N

Hamstall Hall

START 1
The Shoulder of
Mutton

River Blithe

WALK 12;
HAMSTALL
RIDWARE

6

Hamstall
Ridware

Blythe
House
Farm

Hunger △ 5
Hill

Upper
Nethertown
Farm

2

3

Nethertown
Farm

Nethertown

4

Pipe Ridware

River Trent

Church
Farm

TRENT VALLEY

A513

0   ½   1
              km

4. Turn left to walk to a junction at Pipe Ridware. Nearby a little chapel has been converted into a theatre. Before the junction, enter the field on your right by way of the large gates. Follow the hedge on the left as it rises. Towards the top cut right as waymarked to a stile in the next boundary.

5. Once across go right to cross another stile and then to climb the bluff to the left of the old scar and crescent of hawthorns. Go over a stile and continue ahead over two others and through a pocket of woodland. You should now be able to see the triangulation point at the summit of Hunger Hill. Head just to the right of it and then towards a signpost to the left of a house. Cross the stile here and walk along the track.

6. Go right over a stile after the entrance drive. Once in the field turn left and follow this along the hedge. At the corner go left and descend to the village, crossing another stile and then exiting onto the road in the village. Turn right.

```
┌──────────────────────────────────────────────────────┐
│                                                        │
│                    13. Hanbury                         │
│                                                        │
└──────────────────────────────────────────────────────┘
```

Route: Draycott-in-the-Clay — Rough Hays — Hanbury — Foxholes — Draycott

Distance: 3 miles (5km)

Map: OS Pathfinder Abbots Bromley 851

Start: Village Stores on the main road in Draycott

Access: Draycott is served by buses from Uttoxeter on Monday to Saturday. Travel on the A40 to Derby then turn right at Sudbury onto the A515 road to Draycott. There is limited on street parking in the village.

The Cock Inn. 01283 813263

The Cock was one of the many buildings destroyed in the area by the underground explosion at Fauld during the Second World War. The story is told on a notice board outside the pub. The landlord is used to ramblers calling and receives many enquiries about the explosion. There is a circular waymarked walk to the crater which is easy to follow. The Cock is a very welcoming pub with a compact traditional bar complete with roaring fire in winter, a lounge and a family room. There is also a large garden outside so is a popular haunt in summer. Usual opening times are 12pm – 3pm and 6.30pm – 11pm. It is open all day Saturday and Sunday. Meals served 12pm – 3pm and 7pm – 8.30pm evenings all week and all day at weekends. Filled rolls are always available at all opening times. Kimberley Classic from Hardys and Hansons are available on handpull; this is a welcome change in an area which is dominated by large breweries.

Hanbury

Sitting on a hillside above the Trent, Hanbury is a very pleasant village which grew up on the edge of the Forest of Needwood. It was rocked by a massive explosion at Fauld on a winter's morning in

Water pump, Hanbury

1944, but is now a tranquil backwater nestled around the towering church of St Werburgh. King Ethelred appointed his niece, the future St Werburgh, to become the prioress of a nunnery founded here in the 7th century. It was ransacked by the Danes two centuries later and unfortunately there are no ruins remaining. The church is medieval in origin and was tastefully restored by our Victorian ancestors in the last century. It contains the alabaster effigy of a cross-legged knight, thought to be Sir John de Hanbury who died in 1303, a fine example of alabaster work.

The Walk

1. Begin the walk from the Village Stores and Post Office at Draycott in the Clay, a village on the very edge of Needwood Forest. Turn right to walk along the pavement and road to the Swan Inn. Walk through the car park into a field and continue ahead to a stile. Cross here and climb the field to a stile set in a thick hedge exiting onto a road.

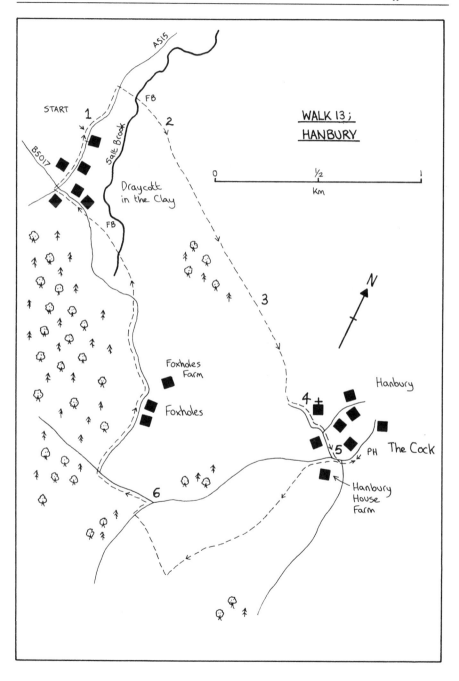

2. Go across the road to enter another field and keep company with a hedge to your left as you rise to pass a water trough. Cross a stile a little higher up the bank and, once over, continue ahead towards the impressive landmark of Hanbury church.

3. As the hedge bears left keep ahead crossing fencing by double gates. This is a very large field which unfolds into a small valley. Keep ahead to a stile, the one nearest the hillside to your left known as Rough Hays. It cannot be seen until you are part way across the field. Cross the stile and continue up the bank by the wooded clough. Cross a stile by a gate and walk along a track. There is a house to your left and the church beyond.

4. Cross a stile by a gate and turn left to walk by a thatched house and by Hanbury Church. Notice the old pump and tie ring for horses. The water tower, which can also be seen for miles around, stands nearby. The lane leads right to a junction by the old school. Keep ahead and then go next left for the Cock public house.

5. Return to the junction by the old school. Turn left into Wood Lane and look for a stile on the left beyond Hanbury House Farm. Cross a field to a stile by a barred gate and then bear slightly right to join a hedgerow. Go over the stile and footbridge, then turn slightly right again through a narrow enclosure to cross another stile. Head for the top right corner and continue through the barred gate ahead. At the signpost by the water trough, turn right to go through a gate and then walk ahead to cross a stile. Keep ahead to a gate which exits onto a road.

6. Turn right, go left at the first junction and then right at the next into a narrow thoroughfare known as Greaves lane. Pass by cottages and the drive to Foxholes Farm beneath a wooded knoll bearing the same name. The road soon drops down by woodland and as it bends left, go ahead over a stile. Follow the stream until you cross the footbridge at the meadow's end. Go over a stile and head slightly left up the bank and ahead towards the houses at Draycott. Join the road and turn right into the village. At the junction go ahead to the main road passing to the right of the old village hall dating from 1845.

---
14. Haughton

Route: Haughton – Haughtondale – Shut Heath – Haughton

Distance: 3 miles (5km)

Map: OS Pathfinder 850 Stafford

Start: The Bell, Haughton

Access: Travel on the main A518 Stafford to Newport road. There is limited on-street parking in the village, so please park considerately. There is a regular bus service from Stafford.

The Bell. 01785 780301

Situated on the main Newport Road, The Bell has been a firm favourite with locals for many years and a Good Beer Guide entry for some time. It is a one room pub which enjoys a good atmosphere. Usual opening times are 11.30am – 2.30pm and 6pm – 11pm. Meals are served 12pm – 2pm. There is an outdoor area and please note that The Bell cannot accommodate young children inside. Pedigree, Banks mild, Marstons Bitter plus one changing guest beer is usually on offer.

Haughton

The village of Haughton features a mixture of old and new, having been mentioned in the Domesday Book as Haltone, a settlement amidst meadows, which it is to this day. There is a pub at each end of the village, and between can be found shops, farms, and a splendid 16th century timbered manor house. The church dates originally from medieval times but has been much restored throughout the centuries. It is interesting that in the 18th century and for the best part of the 19th century this was a red brick structure. The church was rebuilt in the 1880s simply because it was considered

16th century Manor House, Haughton

not to be fitting. Now, we would be delighted by either! This easy going ramble starts from the Bell, just a hop along the main road.

The Walk

1. Turn right and walk along to the church. Enter the churchyard from the main road to pass by the rich red sandstone tower of the Victorian era. Go through a kissing gate, at the other end of the churchyard, onto a road. Turn right and then first left into Brazenhill Lane. Once out of the village you will see Mayo Farm ahead but well before go right along a track with a concrete base. Pass a waterworks and cross a stile into a large field. There is a good view from here of the tree-lined Berry Hill ancient fort.

2. Head diagonally left across the field to cross-fencing. Then con-

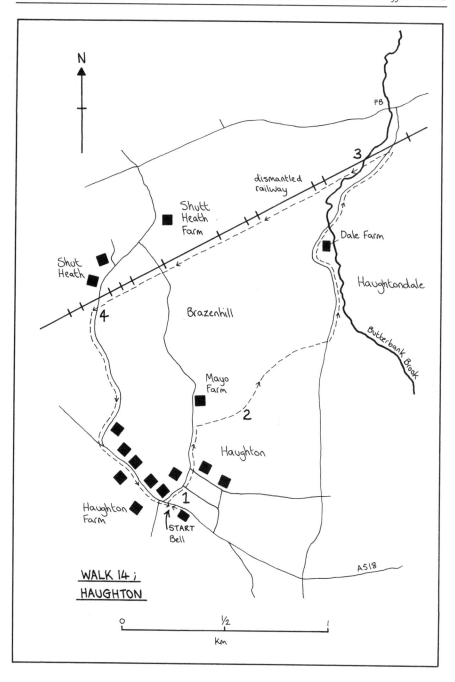

N

FB

3

dismantled
railway

Shutt
Heath
Farm

Dale Farm

Shut
Heath

Haughtondale

4

Brazenhill

Butterbank Brook

Mayo
Farm

2

Haughton

Haughton
Farm

1

START
Bell

A518

WALK 14 ;
HAUGHTON

0   ½   1
Km

tinue slightly right across the next lush pasture. Go over a stile by a gate. Turn left to walk along a quiet lane at Haughtondale until you reach the old railway bridge, at one time the Stafford to Newport and Telford railway. Follow the path, on the other side of the bridge, up to what is now called The Greenway, a walking and cycling route out of Stafford. This will lead eventually to Newport as part of the National Cycle Network.

3. Walk for nearly a mile until you reach a large overbridge and the scant remains of Haughton Station. This would have been a busy little rural spot with passengers coming to and fro, freight trains calling to deposit goods, and a local inn nearby to quench the thirst of many a traveller. It all ended in the 1960s and a quietness descended until the Greenway was developed in recent years.

4. Go left through the picnic site to the road and turn right Follow the lane back into Haughton but take care as there is more traffic on this route than Brazenhill Lane. On reaching the main road turn left to return to The Bell.

15. Kingstone

Route: Kingstone – Kingstone Wood – Darcel's Rough – The Mosses – Kingstone

Distance: 3 miles (5km)

Map: OS Pathfinder 851 Abbots Bromley

Start: The Shrewsbury Arms, Kingstone

Access: Kingstone is best approached from the A518 Uttoxeter to Stafford road or from the B5013 from Uttoxeter. It is difficult to reach by bus.

Village scene, Kingstone

The Shrewsbury Arms. 01889 500213

As the name of this roadside hostelry suggests, the village in past times was dominated by the Earls of Shrewsbury who owned substantial tracts of land hereabouts. This pleasant hostelry serves Marston's Pedigree on handpull in a large lounge bar. Usual opening times: lunchtimes are from 12pm – 2pm (but this can be erratic) and 6pm onwards. Food is available. Families are welcome and there is a beer garden at the rear.

Kingstone

The land owned by the Earls of Shrewsbury was broken up in 1918, and few of the original estate dwellings remain. The impressive church stands on high ground, and is dedicated to St John the Baptist, having been rebuilt by the Earl of Shrewsbury in the 19th century. There is a delightful little well nearby which was at one time an important source of water for the villagers.

The Walk

1. Leave from the entrance to the Shrewsbury Arms to turn left. The road dips to a junction and then climbs out of village. It then descends right and passes a turning for Black Road.

2. Look for a bridlegate on the left which leads into a field. Keep ahead with a hedge on your right above the valley. Carry on through a gate into Kingstone wood. The path runs along the hedge at first, and becomes a wet track through the wood. Keep ahead, avoiding tracks off to the left. Proceed through the opening to the right and then descend to a gate and stile, with a pool on your left.

3. Go through them both and keep ahead. Walk along the old track which rises up through fields, approximately ahead. It then curves slightly left between poles to go through a gate. Follow the field hedge on the right upwards.

4. At the B5013 road, go left. It is best to cross to face the traffic for the short section of roadside walking. Before the road bends to

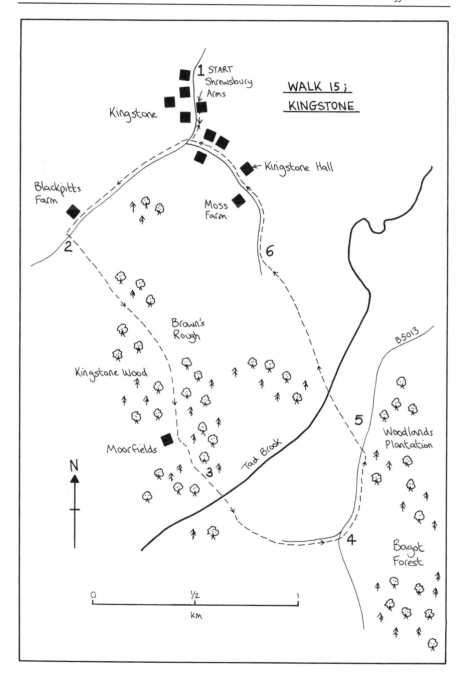

1 START
Shrewsbury
Arms

Kingstone

WALK 15;
KINGSTONE

← Kingstone Hall

Blackpitts
Farm

Moss
Farm

2

6

Brown's
Rough

Kingstone Wood

B5013

Moorfields

5

Woodlands
Plantation

3

Tad Brook

N

4

Bagot
Forest

0   ½
                    km

the right, cross back again when you see a hedgerow running down the field on the left. Look for a stile over the stump of a tree.

5. Head slightly right across the field towards Darcel's Rough. Cross stiles and a footbridge over the Tad Brook. Head in the same direction up the field towards the edge of Kingstone wood, but do not enter here. Instead, go through a gateway.

6. Kingstone church can be seen ahead and is your landmark. You will see a track in the wood on the left, and a dwelling known as The Mosses. You continue ahead to the bottom field corner to enter the track. Then go right to follow it into the village.

16. Kinver

Route: Kinver – Stourbridge – Stewponey – Kinver

Distance: 7 miles (11km)

Map: OS Pathfinder 933 Stourbridge

Start: Traveller's Joy, High Street

Access: This is a linear walk so we recommend use of the bus to travel to your starting point. The Stowbridge to Kinver bus service runs daily. Travel on the A449 to the Stewponey Inn then look for signs on the right to Kinver. There are car parks in the village.

The Plough & Harrow. 01384 872659

The exceptional taste of Batham's Black Country beer is worth a journey to Kinver. The light-coloured and slightly fruity bitter complements the dark brown mild, both of which are much in demand in the West Midlands. The Plough and Harrow serves an excellent pint of both in convivial company. Usual opening times are 12pm – 3pm (not Monday to Thursday) and 7pm – 11pm, but openings depend on the weather. Bar snacks and meals are available from 7pm – 9pm and Saturday and Sunday lunch. Families are welcome if the children are well behaved and there is an outdoor area to the rear of the pub. Movie star pictures decorate the lounge walls so you can gaze over a pint, attempting to guess exactly who they all are. The front bar is far less demanding. The pub is known as 'The Steps' by locals. As this is a linear walk, the pub we recommend in Stourbridge is also a Batham's hostelry, The Royal Exchange in Enville Street, not very far from the bus stop. The front entrance leads to a traditional bar on the left where you will find tiled floors, benches and seats around the fire. In this respect the pub is entirely unspoilt. The beers from Bathams are marvellous.

The Rock Houses, Kinver

Kinver

The southernmost tip of Staffordshire happens to be the high ground of Kinver Edge, an area of wood and heath, where there are great views across several counties. Here you will find the Rock Houses, dwellings carved out of the soft red sandstone. It is hard to imagine but the last of the dwellings was inhabited as late as the 1950s. They have been restored by the National Trust and access is usually available to the grounds during daylight hours. There are several walks to and from the Edge involving several climbs. There are also numerous well-worn paths here so you can easily vary your path to suit. Thus, many still travel to Kinver to explore the high ground above the village but there is much more. Kinver itself was featured in the Domesday Book, as Chenevare, most probably derived from 'keun' and 'vaur' meaning a great ridge. It was certainly known to Iron Age humans, as the scant earthworks of a fort remain.

Kinver has also had an industrial past mainly generated by the arrival of the Staffordshire and Worcestershire Canal. Much of the early industry was related to the production of wool, then iron, flax-making, hatting, and glove making. Kinver Crystal Glass is still produced in the village. Considerable business in this century has related to tourism and recreation. The Kinver Light Railway, for example, existed from 1900 bringing visitors from the industrial Black Country to what was described as 'the Switzerland of the Midlands'. You can still see the old trackbed in places even though it was dismantled in the 1930s. Most folk walked up to the Edge but as now many were attracted to the history and charm of the High Street which features 17th and 18th century dwellings. At the far end on the road to the church is the finest building in the village, the half-timbered Old Grammar School House which won an Architectural Heritage award in 1975.

The Walk

1. Step One is to catch the bus on the High Street through to Stourbridge. Ask for the last stop on Enville Street (main A458) where you will find the Royal Exchange which happens to be open all day. Then make your way, around the corner on the left, to the Bonded Warehouse on the Stourbridge Branch canal. This is a handsome 18th century Grade II listed warehouse and much of the wharf here has been beautifully restored. There are several boats moored but it is not easy to gain access to the canal towpath. You will most probably have to continue along Amblecote Road, which becomes High Street, to a set of traffic lights. On the right is Holy Trinity church where several famous glassmakers are buried.

2. At the Royal Doulton Crystal works, turn left into Wollaston Road and at the canal bridge go right to walk down to the towpath of the Stourbridge Arm. Continue ahead along the canal, through an industrial zone where boats would have delivered raw materials to the doorways that are now bricked up.

3. On reaching Wordsley Junction, cross the bridge and turn left. To the right is Wordsley Church, with the Stourbridge Canal

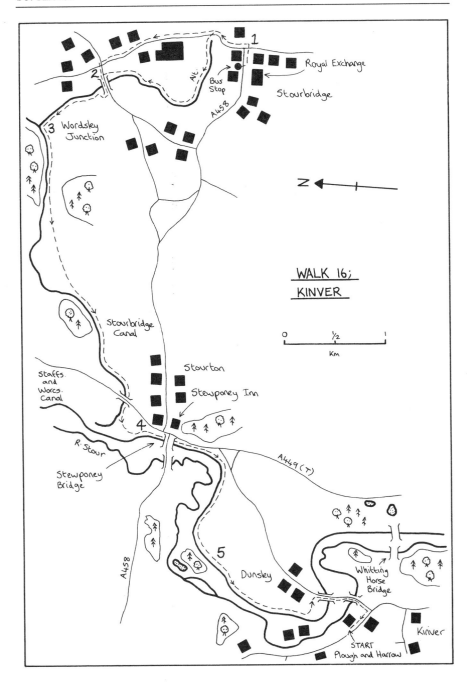

Royal Exchange

Stourbridge

1

Bus
Stop
Alt.
A458

2

3 Wordsley
Junction

Z ←——

WALK 16;
KINVER

0   ½   1
Km

Stourbridge
Canal

Stourton

Stewponey Inn

Staffs.
and
Worcs.
Canal

4

R. Stour

A449 (T)

Stewponey
Bridge

A458

5

Dunsley

Whitting
Horse
Bridge

Kinver

START
Plough and Harrow

rising up through locks. The remainder of the walk is straightforward. Follow the canal to Stourton where you can leave the canal to walk through the village and call at the Stewponey Inn. You can then regain the towpath near the old Stewponey Bridge which carried the tramway. Otherwise stay on the towpath to reach the Staffordshire and Worcestershire Canal and cross to join the other side.

4. Either way you have to turn left along the towpath of the Staffordshire and Worcestershire Canal, a fine example of the work of James Brindley, built to follow the contour of the land. Nearby is Stourton Castle which was maintained as a hunting lodge when the entire area was covered by Kinver Forest and hunted by nobility. The house you see now is primarily Victorian.

5. The section through to Kinver passes through beautiful countryside and offers good views of the trackbed of the Kinver Light Railway. You approach the village at Dunsley Bridge, where there is a pub on the left and the waterworks to the right. Leave the canal here to go right back into High Street.

17. Lapley

Route: Lapley – Lapley Wood Farm – Wheaton Aston – Lapley

Distance: 2½ miles (4km)

Map: OS Pathfinder 871 Cannock (North)

Start: The Hartley Arms, Wheaton Aston

Access: Penkridge and Wolverhampton to Wheaton Aston. Travel by the A5 looking for signs to Wheaton Aston. There is limited on street car parking in the village.

The Vaughan Arms. 01785 840325

The Vaughan is in a lovely setting at Lapley. Inside, it is divided into a number of areas at two levels, served by one main bar. It was named after well-known local people, the Vaughan family, who

The Vaughan Arms

lived in Lapley House, directly opposite the pub. Originally the pub was situated behind Lapley House. The noise was unbearable at closing time so it is now housed at two converted cottages on its present site. It is a friendly community pub and funds are raised through the Harvest festival celebration, for example. There are live music nights every other Tuesday. Usual opening times are Monday to Friday 12pm – 3pm and 7pm – 11pm. Saturday 12pm – 4pm and 6.30pm – 11pm. Hot and cold meals served every lunch and evening. Monday to Friday 12pm – 2.30pm and 7pm – 9pm. Saturday 12pm – 2.30pm and 6.30pm – 9.30pm. Sunday 12pm – 2pm and 7pm – 9pm. Families are welcome and there are benches on front patio where you will find lovely blooms in the summer months. Marstons Bitter and Pedigree, Banks's Bitter, Old Speckled Hen, and Marstons Head Brewers Choice, are usually available as well as other guest beers.

Lapley

Lapley Church is easily recognised by its very large central tower which illustrates that it was much more significant in previous centuries. It dates mainly from the 12th century and has an interesting interior. There are a number of fine buildings in the village including Park House which exhibits unusual castellations such as the gatehouse and turrets. Lapley Hall is a splendid red-brick building, with tall chimneys. Lapley Manor, by the church and on the site of the old Benedictine Priory, and Lapley Court are two timber-framed houses of great character. This ramble features a tale of two villages, Wheaton Aston which has grown and Lapley which has undoubtedly stayed much the same since the 17th century. Wheaton Aston is now very much a dormitory community but still retains a number of features such as the Hartley Arms (Banks's beers), standing by the Shropshire Union canal. It makes a good starting point for the ramble.

The Walk

1. From the Hartley Arms, turn right over the aptly-named Tavern Bridge, noticing the old weight restriction sign. Bear right at the

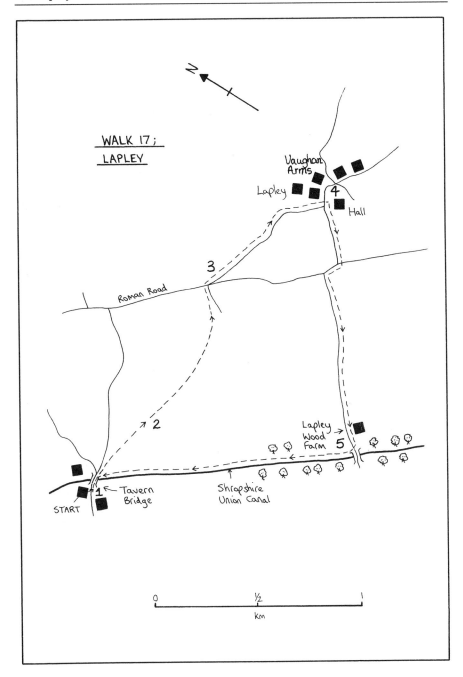

WALK 17;
LAPLEY

Vaughan
Arms
Lapley
4
Hall

3

Roman Road

2

Lapley
Wood
Farm
5

1 Tavern
Bridge
START

Shropshire
Union Canal

0   ½   1
km

fork. Pass by a few cottages and look for a stile on the right which leads to a rugby pitch. Go diagonally left across the field to a far corner where another stile is crossed then follow the banks of a stream to a footbridge.

2. Once over, turn left but within a few paces, head slightly right across a stile midfield. Cross this and keep in the same direction to a gateway leading on to a lane – there is a footpath sign by the fencing.

3. Lapley church can be seen more clearly and this is the mid-way point of the walk, with the Vaughan Arms around the corner. Turn right on to the lane, a Roman road at one time, and then left at the junction. This lane leads to the lovely church of Lapley, said to have been part of a Benedictine monastic settlement; the remains, dating back to the 11th century, are to be found mainly in surrounding houses. The central tower dominates and, while a lack of transepts seems unusual for a country church, it is, without doubt an inspiring feature on the landscape. Be sure to close the gate when leaving the churchyard for the lush grass is kept short by a flock who have a habit of wandering!

4. Continue along the lane to the corner by the old hall. Go left for the Vaughan Arms, otherwise, turn right here to join the Staffordshire Way and walk along the field's edge to exit into what appears to be an old road. Turn right to walk a few paces to the new road and cross over to continue along a farm access track. Follow this to the farmyard of Lapley Wood Farm, often with dogs yapping, and through to a short green lane which brings you, by way of a gate, to a canal bridge.

5. Just before, turn right to join the towpath of this splendid navigation and walk ahead to Wheaton Aston. Don't be surprised if you put a heron or two to flight along here for they seem to like this habitat. Walk up to the road at the bridge, for a return to the Hartley Arms.

18. Longdon

Route: Longdon – Hill Top Farm – Longdon Church – Longdon

Distance: 2 miles (3km)

Map: OS Pathfinder 872 Rugeley and Lichfield (North)

Start: The Swan with Two Necks

Access: There is a regular bus between Stafford and Lichfield which serves the village, including on Sundays. Longdon is on the A51 road. There is limited car parking in the village.

The Swan with Two Necks. 01543 490251

This is 400-year-old pub with five traditional open fires and low beamed ceilings which make it a rather enchanting place on a winter's day. The bar has a stone flagged floor and there is a restaurant too. Usual opening hours: 12pm – 2.30pm and 7pm – 11pm. Food served 12pm – 2pm and 7pm – 9.30pm. Families with children over 14 are welcome and there is a beer garden. On handpull are Ansells Bitter and Mild, Burton Ale, and Burton Bridge, plus a guest beer.

Longdon

Longdon is best known for nearby Beaudesert Hall which was originally a palace of Bishops but now lies in ruins. Grand Lodge on Borough Lane, dates from the early 19th century, and was one of several lodges built on the edge of what was once an enclosed park. The most other endearing feature in the village is the church which stands a little way from the nucleus of houses nestled around the village green. It is veritable source of local history.

The Walk

1. From the Swan with Two Necks, go left, as signposted along a road known as Ford Lane. Inevitably, this leads down to a ford, but the path runs along to a footbridge. Keep ahead along a track, which can get muddy, by a brook.

2. Go through a gate, and then keep right. Continue ahead part way along a field but when you see the stump of an old telegraph pole on the left, turn right up the field following what was an old hedge. You will see an old tree trunk between hedges ahead and the church on the right in the distance. Follow the old track up the hillside and at the top keep right at the junction of tracks.

3. You approach the buildings of Hill Top Farm. Before a thatched cottage on the corner, go through a wooden barred gate; the path is signposted. Keep ahead along the hedge to cross a stile. Go ahead to a barred gate but do not go through it but instead go left along the hedge. Cross the stile and go through a small enclosure to another. Cherry Orchard farm can be seen to left.

4. Go slightly right across a field. You can see the pinnacles of the church tower. Go to very top right corner where a small metal gate enters the next field. Go left and head just to the left of the church and here you will find a gateway into the churchyard and graffiti on wall dating from 1904. There are a number of fascinating headstones including the one belonging to the Swainston Adamson Family. He was involved in the design and construction of the Bore Ghant Incline in Bombay and the Great Indian Peninsula Railway from Sholopore to Hyberabad, from 1860 to

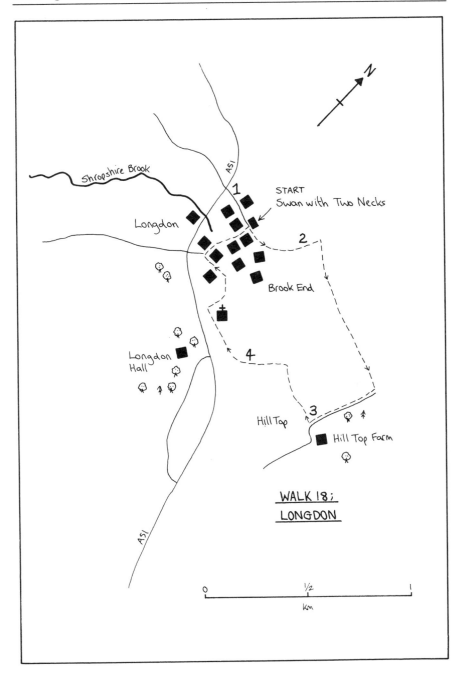

START
Swan with Two Necks

Shropshire Brook

Longdon

1

2

Brook End

4

Longdon
Hall

Hill Top

3

Hill Top Farm

WALK 18;
LONGDON

0   ½   1
km

1879. Go to the right of the church and exit by a gate at far corner. Go through field ahead to houses. Then bear left before the next gate and through another kissing gate. This leads down to rear of the Longdon Club. Turn right for The Swan with Two Necks.

19. Marchington

Route: Marchington Church – Stock Lane – Woodroffe's – Marchington Cliff – Marchington

Distance: 5 miles (8km)

Maps: OS Pathfinder 831 Uttoxeter and 851 Abbots Bromley

Start: Marchington Church

Access: By Bus: there is a bus from Uttoxeter on Mondays to Saturdays. By car: follow the B5017 road from Uttoxeter to Marchington. The village is signposted off this road. There is limited on-street parking.

The Bulls Head. 01283 820358

The Bulls Head is a homely and traditional pub which has served the village well over the years. The entrance is through very traditional wooden and glass doors not much seen these days and walkers are very welcome. Usual opening times: Monday to Friday, 12pm – 2pm and 5.30pm – 11pm; Saturday, 12pm – 2.30pm and 6pm – 11pm. Light snacks are available but the emphasis in the pub is on the excellent beer – Pedigree, and a Marstons guest beer. There is no family room and the pub is not very suitable for children.

Marchington

Lying on the rising slopes of the Dove Valley the village of Marchington is the starting point for this four mile hike to Marchington Woodlands, one of the prettiest corners of the county. Marchington is a village steeped in tradition and folklore as well as having a number of distinctive buildings, particularly the handsome 17th century hall in the centre of the village. Start your ramble from Marchington church, an unusual red-brick building standing at the end of an avenue of trees. It has an octagonal tower and a dome. In early times it was known as 'Maercham', and is recorded in an Anglo

Saxon document dated AD 951. For the best part of its existence it has been agrarian and time has moved slowly in these parts. In past centuries, Marchington gained quite a reputation for its treatment of wife beaters. The perpetrator was set astride a pole and marched through the village by the local constable or crier who duly shouted to all and sundry the bad deeds.

The Hall, Marchington

The Walk

1. From the gateway to the church, turn right to walk through the village, passing the Dog and Partridge public house. Cross a brook and turn right to the old almshouses and Marchington Hall. The road you are on, Jacks Lane, curves left and then continues ahead. Pass a turning to Woodlands View and a signpost on the left to Church Road. After approximately 20 metres, look for a stile by a gate. Cross here.

2. Do not go ahead up the field but bear slightly right across to a stile in a hedge. Once over, keep ahead through another small pasture to a stile exiting onto the B5017 road. Look for two stiles on the other side which lead into a field where horses are kept. The next section of the walk traverses a number of low-lying fields to Stocks Lane.

3. Follow the fence ahead to cross a stile. Go straight on to cross two more stiles and go ahead again through a small enclosure to a ditch and stile. Once over, continue to a footbridge and stile. Then head slightly right to a stile which stands to the right of a hawthorn bush and a stream.

4. Join the narrow road known as Stock Lane. Turn left and follow this past Stocklane Farm and then rise to Higher Stocklane farm. Just beyond is a stile on the right. Cross it and walk ahead, with the farm on your right, to another stile by a gate. Now, go diagonally right over the field to a stile and onward in a similar direction to a stile beneath hawthorns. Continue likewise to the next stile beneath a tall hedge. Once through, head slightly right, aiming for the far-right corner. Do not go through the gateway onto the road. Instead turn left to keep company with the hedge on your right, which runs parallel to the road until you reach a stile on the right which leads onto Hodge Lane. This type of path is usually associated with a busier thoroughfare from long ago, when carts and wagons churned up the road so much that it rendered the way impassable for travellers on foot. In such circumstances a path used to be created a few metres away from the thoroughfare to render it walkable.

5. The road rises to pass the half-timbered Jacobean residence known as Woodroffe's, after the person who originally built it in the 17th century. Just past the house on the left is a gateway leading into a large field. Go through here and head for the far right corner, there being two remaining trees as a landmark. Cross a stile before the corner. Once through the hedge bear left and cross a stile in the corner. The views of Marchington Woods are good from this vantage point. Continue along the top of the bank for a few paces but then cut right down the field heading for the

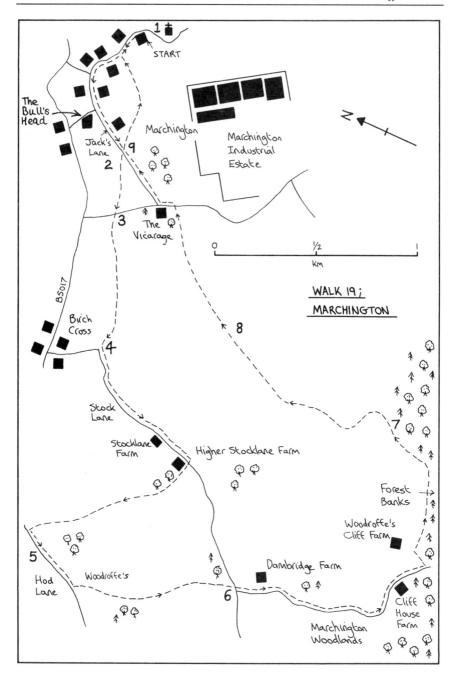

START

The
Bull's
Head

Marchington

Marchington
Industrial
Estate

N

Jack's
Lane

9

2

3

The
Vicarage

B5017

0   ½   1
km

WALK 19;
MARCHINGTON

Birch
Cross

4

8

Stock
Lane

Stocklane
Farm

Higher Stocklane Farm

7

Forest
Banks

Woodroffe's
Cliff Farm

5

Hod
Lane

Woodroffe's

Dambridge Farm

6

Cliff
House
Farm

Marchington
Woodlands

house before the road junction below. There is a stile in the hedge just to the left of the house. Cross it and bear right.

6. At the junction, go left and follow the lane through the scattered houses of Marchington Woodlands. Pass Cliff House Farm on the right and continue to climb towards the woods. Turn left after Cliff Cottage down a green lane which winds its way along the edge of the woodlands for approximately half a mile. Look for a finger post pointing left through a small gate into a field. Go through it.

7. Walk ahead across the field to join a cross-track near the opposite hedge. Go right and go through a gate. There is a good view back to Marchington Woodlands church from here. Keep ahead on the tractor track to go through another gate. This leads to another gate. Go through it but now leave the track by heading slightly left to a stile which cannot be seen at first. It is approximately a third of the way along the boundary from the right corner. Once through, head in a similar direction to another hidden stile in a thick-set hedge, about 100 metres back from the far corner. Be patient for this is not easy to find until you are near it!

8. Go over the footbridge and stile. Turn right and cross the field to a stile in a hedge. Cross it and the footbridge. Then go slightly right through the next pasture to a stile which stands to the right of the trees. Cross the stile and continue ahead to a stile by a post. Walk ahead to a stile by a gate and exit onto the main road. Turn left and then next right to retrace your steps towards the village but cut right between houses as signposted to Church Road. This well-worn path cuts across a pasture to a stile to the left of a house. Cross the track and continue to skirt a hedge on the right around to a footbridge over the brook.

9. Once over go left to cross another stile and to meet another path coming in from the left. Keep ahead along the stream. Please be considerate as you pass houses to join the road. Go right to the church.

20. Marston

Route: Marston – Aquamoor – Burnt Withys – Lower Brockhurst – Marston

Distance: 4 miles (6km)

Map: OS Pathfinder 871 Cannock North

Start: The Fox, Marston

Access: There is a limited bus service between Wolverhampton and Penkridge which serves Marston. Car access should be by way of Wheaton Aston off the A5 road.

The Fox. 01785 840729

This amazing survivor has enjoyed a reputation for years in supplying a choice of real ales and traditional ciders. There is still a good choice here with beers such as Charles Wells Eagle bitter, Mansfield Old Bailey, Woods Wonderful, plus several other guest beers. There is usually a cider from Westons of Herefordshire available also. There are two rooms and a restaurant at The Fox and it relies almost entirely on trade from away as the hamlet consists of only a few dwellings. Usual opening times are 12pm – 2pm and 7pm – 11pm Tuesday to Saturday but please note that the pub is closed all day Monday. Open Sunday 12pm – 2pm and 7pm – 10.30pm. Traditional bar snacks are served. Families are welcome and the pub has a garden to the rear. Walkers are welcome to leave cars on the car park whilst going for a walk (at their own risk).

Marston

Marston is an agricultural community just to the west of Wheaton Aston. It is a favourite spot with cyclists but less so with ramblers, mainly because so many of the paths hereabouts suffer from all

Checking the paths near Marston

manner of obstructions, from crops and barbed wire. Therefore, we are delighted to include this one!

The area has always been known for its cereal crops, hence the name Wheaton Aston, but there are also many grazing pastures. Before extensive drainage of the fields and recent dry summers, the area was known for its small pools and streams, especially Motty Meadows, and other wet areas. They attracted all manner of wildlife. Most have been lost to agricultural improvement.

The Walk

1. Start from The Fox. Go right to walk along the road out of the hamlet. The road bends right and then left to reach a group of houses at Aquamoor. Bear left, by a dwelling named Homestead, along the drive to soon reach Aquamoor Farm. Just beyond the track bears left but you continue ahead over a stile.

2. Keep ahead for approximately 200 metres where you cross a stile

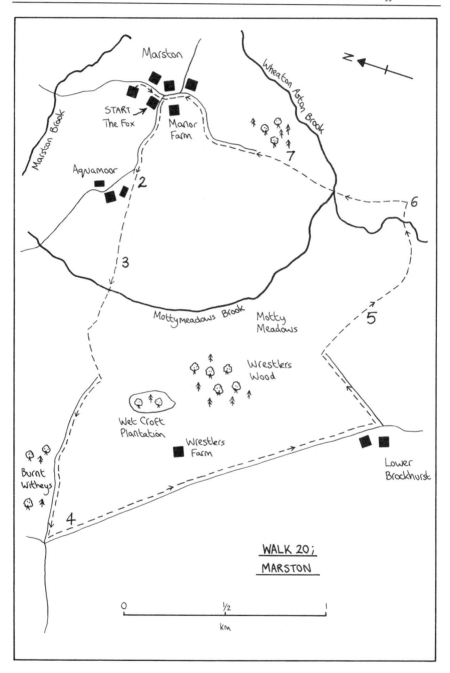

Marston

Wheaton Aston Brook

Marston Brook

START
The Fox

Manor
Farm

7

Aquamoor

2

6

3

Mottymeadows Brook   Motty
Meadows

5

Wrestlers
Wood

Wet Croft
Plantation

Wrestlers
Farm

Lower
Brockhurst

Burnt
Witheys

4

WALK 20;
MARSTON

0   ½   1

km

on the right. Then keep left to walk through the pasture to a boundary which you cross. Continue ahead to cross a drainage ditch, then through a hedge and over the stream again.

3. The way should be slightly right to cross the stream again and into an old cartway. This leads up to a junction. Go right and follow the old track up to pass a woodland, Burnt Withys to a road. This track is a real haven for plant and wildlife. In the summer there are several varieties of butterflies to be seen among the thistle, roadside flowers such as campion and speedwort, and feathery grasses.

4. At the road, go left. It is nearly a mile along the tree lined highway to Lower Brockhurst farm. Go left opposite the farm buildings along a track, signposted as a bridleway. The track bends right to enter a field. Keep ahead to go through a gap in the next hedge. The path now follows an overgrown remnant of a track which is truncated mid field. Continue in a similar direction.

5. Head for a section of fencing. There is a clump of trees behind it and to the right stands Bent Farm. Cross the fencing and a track. To the left is a gate with a notice 'Fish Pool car park'. Go left over the cattle grid and then cut right again. You may wonder if this is really meant to be a bridleway!

6. Walk ahead along hedge, ignoring a barred gate on the right, until you reach a tractor bridge. Once over go ahead towards a gateway but beforehand turn left to walk up the field. Keep company with this right hand boundary to the very top corner of the field. You will see before a tempting bridle gate and way to your right. This is a lovely route through to Wheaton Aston but perhaps it is for another walk.

7. At the top of the field, go through the barred gate and over the tractor bridge. Head slightly right up the field to a gateway in the top right corner. This leads to a track, often muddy, which leads back to Marston. Go left at the road and left again for The Fox.

21. Newborough

Route: Newborough – Holt Hill – Rushton's Hill – Holly Bush – Newborough

Distance: 3 miles (5km)

Map: OS Pathfinder Abbots Bromley 851

Start: The Red Lion, Newborough

Access: There is a limited bus service to Newborough from Burton. Travel on the A40 to Sudbury then the A515 towards Lichfield. Newborough is signposted right at Six Roads End.

The Red Lion. 01283 575259

This traditional old pub at the centre of the village has a good bar, a smaller lounge and a fairly spacious dining room. It is often decorated with fresh flowers and ramblers are welcome here. Usual opening times: Monday to Saturday, 12pm – 3pm and 6pm – 11pm. Food is served Monday to Saturday, 12pm – 2pm, and 7pm – 9.30pm. Families are welcome and there is a pleasant garden to the rear. Marstons Pedigree and Marstons Bitter are usually available on handpump.

Newborough

Lying in the ancient forest of Needwood, Newborough is clustered around the impressive looking parish church. It has an octagonal tower and a spire which can be seen for miles around. It is chronicled that it stands on the site of a former inn, The White Hart. The village is known for its annual well dressing celebrations but otherwise is not much visited despite being in the heart of delightful countryside. Its earlier name was the New Borough of Agardsley, derived from Edgarslege, meaning Edgar's pasture, of Saxon origin. The new name relates to medieval times when a 'New Borough' was

A weary walker at the well

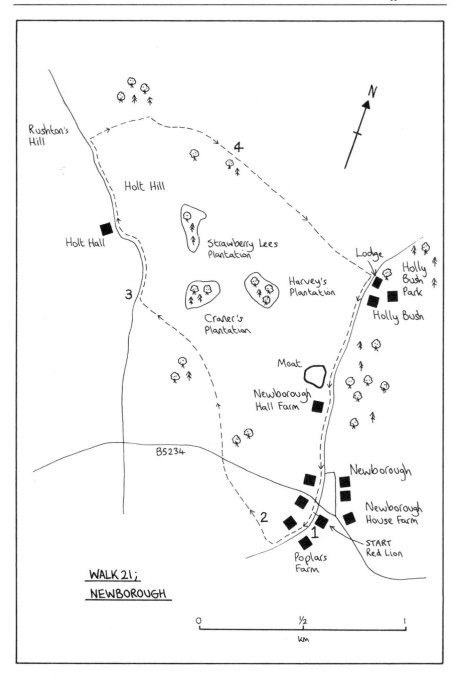

Rushton's Hill

Holt Hill

Holt Hall

Strawberry Lees Plantation

Harvey's Plantation

Craner's Plantation

3

Lodge

Holly Bush Park

Holly Bush

Moat

Newborough Hall Farm

B5234

Newborough

Newborough House Farm

START
Red Lion

2

1

Poplars Farm

N

4

WALK 21;

NEWBOROUGH

0   ½   1

km

set out, and the plots of land in and around the village reflect this early practice of land allocation.

The Walk

1. This ramble is mainly across fields with two short sections of road walking. From the entrance to the churchyard turn right to walk along the Yoxall Road as far as The Buffalo inn and restaurant. Go right through the car park to the rear (by the fuel tank) where you will find a footpath sign and stile leading into the field.

2. Walk up the pasture to cross a stile by a gate. Go over the road with care and cross another stile. Head slightly left across the next field, cross a stile and then continue slightly left to join the edge of a field. Keep ahead to cross another stile and then go ahead through the middle of a field; the path runs just to the left of an electric telegraph pole. Cross the next stile and head towards the roof top of a house on the horizon, in a slightly right direction. Cross a stile by a barred gate onto a road. Turn right.

3. Pass by Holt Hall Farm. The road dips down and passes a house on the right at Rushton's Hill (no relation to the co author). Just beyond, look for a track on the right, through a gateway. Follow this ahead, with a hedge to your left. Pass a pool on your right part way up the field. Follow the field boundary up to the top corner; bear right and, half way along, go left over a stile. Head slightly right up the field to cross a stile between gates.

4. Turn right to walk through the next pasture where cows and sheep graze. Cross a fence and go ahead again, but you will have to skirt the pool at the next boundary as it is impossible to get through. Follow the hedgeline on your right down to a dip where the infant River Swarbourn flows. Then climb to a stile which exits onto Hollybush Road. You will see Hollybush Farm on your left. Turn right for the village. Note the well in the village dating from 1859, a reminder of the importance of healthy local water supplies in past times.

22. Outwoods

Route: Outwoods – Windmill Bank – Manor Farm – Moreton – Moreton Brook – Outwoods

Distance: 4 miles (6km)

Map: OS Pathfinder 870 Telford

Start: The Village Tavern, Outwoods

Access: Travel on the Stafford, Gnosall and Newport bus to Coley Mill. It is a mile walk to the Village Tavern. Car travellers should look for the signs off the A518 after Gnosall Heath.

The Village Tavern. 01952 691216

Of all the country pubs visited in preparation of this book, the Village Tavern has to be the friendliest hostelries to be found in Staffordshire. Good Beer Guide Entry in 1996 this exceptional country pub has to be visited. There is a small lounge and larger traditional bar which are deservedly popular with walkers and cyclists. Families are welcome and home cooked food is available. Usual opening hours are 12pm – 3pm at the weekends only and usually from 6pm in the summer (7.30pm in winter). Wildmans, named after the landlord, is brewed by Enville Ale, and there are ever changing guest beers here to be found in tip top condition.

Outwoods

Nestled on a small ridge, probably lying on the Spring Line the small hamlet of Outwoods has simply let the world go by. The railway came within a half mile but there was no station. There is also a small chapel but for the most part the scattered farms and dwellings beneath Outwoods Bank have been involved in agriculture through the ages. Nearby Moreton is a larger. The little church dates from

Lost outside the Village Tavern

Norman but is primarily a Victorian restoration undertaken by Trubshaw. It looks across the valley to the Moreton Brook.

The Walk

1. Start from the Village Tavern. Turn right to walk up the hill. The road becomes a track and approaches a bungalow and farm buildings at Outwoodsbank Farm. Go over the stile by a gate on the right and then keep ahead along the fencing to skirt the farm. Cross another stile by a gate to walk ahead by a barn. Then, cut left over a stile and bear right.

2. Leave the farm behind to reach another stile. Once over, follow the hedge on the right to a further stile on the right. Cross over and turn left to walk up the flanks of Windmill Bank. The next stile is on the left beneath an oak tree. Bear right to walk alongside fencing to a metal gate (which is usually tied with string).

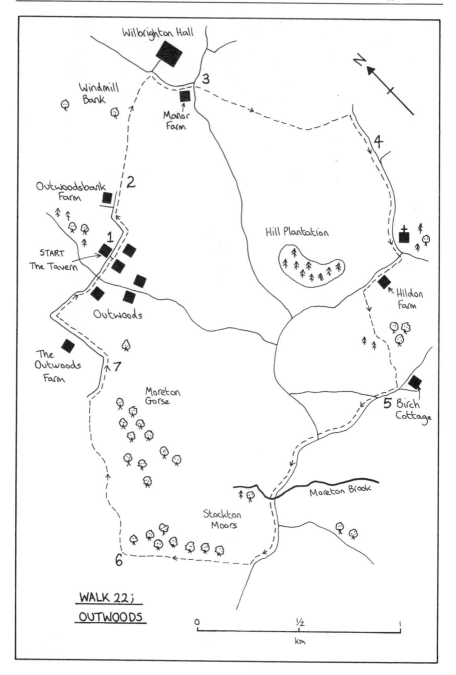

Wilbrighton Hall

Windmill
Bank

3

Manor
Farm

Outwoodsbank
Farm

2

Hill Plantation

4

1

START
The Tavern

Hildon
Farm

Outwoods

The
Outwoods
Farm

7

5 Birch
Cottage

Moreton
Gorse

Moreton Brook

Stockton
Moors

6

WALK 22;
OUTWOODS

0   ½   1

km

Continue ahead through a small enclosure to the right of a dwelling. The path joins a drive and meets a road.

3. Go right. You soon reach a T-junction at Manor Farm. Cross over the road and a stile leads into a very large field often in crop. Head slightly right as indicated by the signpost. Aim for the gate to the left of the pool and go through a small plantation. Keep ahead in the next field, which is equally extensive and usually sown with corn, to the right of a pool and then in a similar direction, passing a secluded pool on the left. Crop obstructions have been reported in the past so hopefully there will be a path through for you. The path heads to an indent in the field where you will see a metal gate and a green track leading up to a road by a dwelling.

4. On the road, turn right to descend by cottages to the old vicarage to Moreton. The church stands to the left on slightly higher ground. You reach a junction where you turn right into Pooley Lane. Pass by the old smithy and opposite a group of houses go left over a stile. This passes through an enclosure to a field. Head slightly right towards the middle point of the trees which happen to hide two pools. The right of way runs through a gap between the pools but can get heavy in growth so a stick would not be amiss. On the other side head to the right of Birch Cottage and you will eventually see a stile leading onto the road.

5. Go right and then at the fork keep left. At the next junction keep ahead along a road signposted to Pave Lane. The road bends left to cross Moreton Brook and then rises and bends right and then left. Go through the left-hand gate and keep company with a hedge to your right and the wood beyond.

6. At the end of the wood, go right through a gate and follow the track ahead. Ignore any turns to the right as you follow this near to the Moreton Brook. As the track bends left, go right through a metal barred gate and follow the fence on the right. Cross a stile and continue ahead. On reaching a gate go right up a track.

7. This soon bends left and then passes by a farm and cottages. Ignore the first turning to the right but go right at the next bend. This leads up to a cross-roads at Outwoods. Go across to return to the Village Tavern Inn.

23. Pattingham

Route: Pattingham – Westbeech – Nurton Hill – Great Moor – The Clive – Pattingham

Distance: 5 miles (8km)

Map: OS Pathfinders 912 Wolverhampton (South) and 891 Wolverhampton (North)

Start: The Crown, Pattingham

Access: There is a bus service on Mondays to Saturdays from Wolverhampton. By car it is possible to travel on the A449, and A454 to Compton then as signposted to Perton and Pattingham. There is car parking near to the church.

The Crown. (0902 700268)

The Crown is a friendly pub which is liked by local people. The bar is always busy and there is a good atmosphere. Usual opening times are Monday to Wednesday, 12pm – 3pm; Thursday and Friday, 12pm – 4pm and Saturday 12pm – 4.30pm. On Monday to Saturday the pub is open in the evenings from 6.30pm onwards. Sandwiches are available from the bar and there are often barbecues in summer. Children are welcome till 9pm and there is a garden. On tap is Directors Bitter, Worthington Best, Draught Bass, Banks Mild plus a guest beer.

Pattingham

The village has several Georgian houses and large villas. The church has a tall spire – a landmark that can be seen for miles around. In 1868 an American, Elihu Burritt, in *"Walks in the Black Country and its Green Border-Land"* wrote "Pattingham, with some of the tall red Midland Queen Anne houses which look so like dolls' houses".

Pattingham village

The Walk

1. Start the walk from The Crown public house. Go right to walk by the church. Turn left and you will see on the left, just beyond the churchyard, the elegant vicarage. Go right through a gap to playing fields. Head straight across to a kissing gate. Turn left along the road to walk out of the village.

2. The road continues to bend right, passing by an entrance to Westbeech House and then Westbeech Farm on the right. Rise up a bank and on the right is a footpath to the right along a track. It is signposted. Keep ahead as the track bears left. Your path narrows, and you simply keep ahead until you reach Nurton Hill Road.

3. Go right to descend towards Nurton Hill but then rise up to a summit where there is a track on the left. Follow this bridleway towards a house but keep to the corralled path which is to the right. This descends to a corner and a lane, Warstone Hill Road. Keep right to descend to the Wolverhampton Road by New Buildings Farm.

4. Cross the road and go left along the wide verge to a stile on the right. Once in the field, head slightly left to a stile. Cross this and keep ahead to enter a small woodland in a marshy area, rich in plantlife and butterflies in summer. It is not easy to pick your way through here but just beyond you will see an opening in the field boundaries. Keep ahead along the right hand hedge to the corner and a gap in the hedge, leading down to a stile of sorts.

5. Cross this and walk over the footbridge to meet a well-worn path. Go right and walk through the valley to Great Moor. Aim for the cottage and follow the path to continue along the drive to a road. Go right to walk down to the junction.

6. Your way is ahead along the ford. In reality the Nurton Brook runs along the road for nearly a quarter of a mile. The lane bears left but you keep ahead. A bridleway sign indicates a route through the gate on the right. The bridleway runs through two fields beneath an edge and the handsome looking Georgian farmhouse of Little Moor. Follow the hedge on the left through

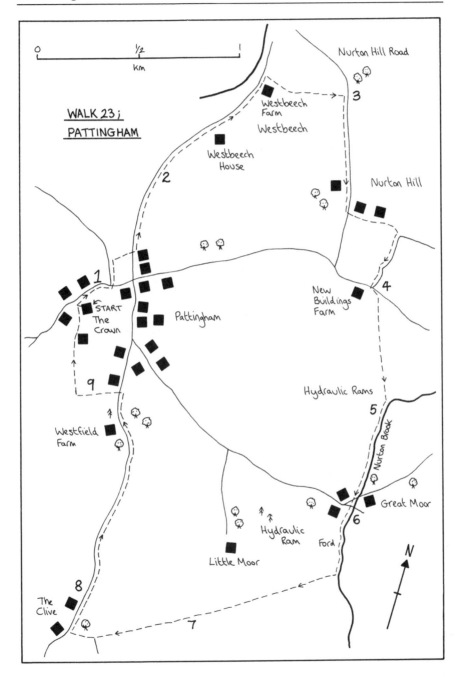

WALK 23 ;
PATTINGHAM

Nurton Hill Road

Westbeech Farm
Westbeech
Westbeech House

Nurton Hill

START
The Crown

Pattingham

New Buildings Farm

Hydraulic Rams

Nurton Brook

Westfield Farm

Great Moor

Hydraulic Ram

Ford

Little Moor

The Clive

N

to a small wood, marked by bridle gates. At the other end it enters an old track and continues ahead to another bridle gate. This section can become overgrown.

7. You continue ahead with the hedge on the right. At the field corner, cross a stile to pursue a well-worn route along the slope of a lovely ridge where kestrels hover in pursuit of small animals. This slight elevation offers great views across to Shropshire, one of the loveliest spots in this part of the county. This gives out at a stile and gate onto a rough track. Go right to walk up the narrow sandstone cutting to a road.

8. Go right to walk by a farm and renovated buildings. Follow the route back towards Pattingham. Be way of the traffic for there is more on this highway than the others used. The church spire is your guide. Enter the village to pass by a garage. On passing a bungalow, Oaklea, look for steps and an ivy clad signpost on the left.

9. Follow this path between gardens and over the field to a small gate by a cottage. On the track go right and this soon joins a residential road. Keep ahead to the main road where you bear right for The Crown.

24. Penkridge

Route: Penkridge—Preston Vale—Mitton—Bickford Meadows—Whiston — Preston Vale — Penkridge

Distance: 8 miles (13km)

Map: OS Pathfinder 871 Cannock (North)

Start: Littleton Arms, Penkridge

Access: Penkridge, on the A449, is served by rail (Mondays-Saturdays) and bus (daily) from Stafford and Wolverhampton.

The Littleton Arms. 01785 712287

The Littleton Arms was at one time a premier coaching house before the arrival of the railway. The stables at the back of the inn are Grade II listed. From here, mail coaches with famous names would travel daily to other parts of England. The Littleton has a number of lounge areas around a central bar and has a restaurant. It is gaining reputation for keeping fine ales and usually on handpull Worthington Best and Bass, Highgate Mild, and guest beers which change on a regular basis.

Penkridge

Penkridge is a busy centre situated on a bridging point over the River Penk. The old part, situated around the church, is well worth exploring. The church dominates what would have been a thriving medieval quarter. It would have been one of the collegiate churches as mentioned in the Gnosall walk and this explains why it would have been larger than a mere parish church. There are many fine monuments inside including those to the Littleton family who were influential in these parts – hence the name of the inn. Nearby are a number of fine Georgian houses including The Rectory and the old deanery. The Littleton Arms is also a handsome addition to the area.

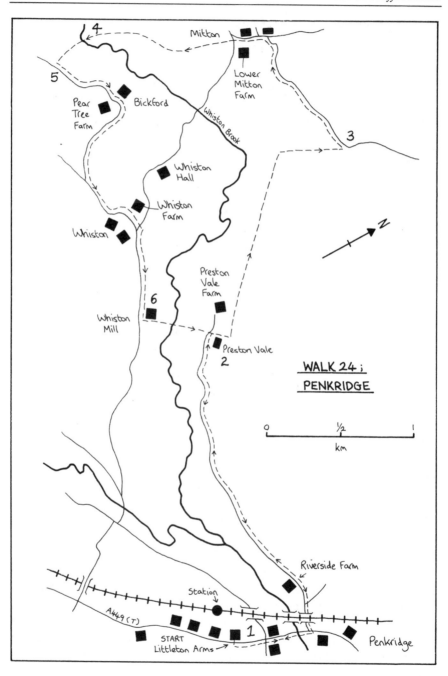

Mitton

Lower
Mitton
Farm

4

5

Pear
Tree
Farm

Bickford

Whiston Brook

Whiston
Hall

Whiston
Farm

Whiston

3

N

Preston
Vale
Farm

6

Whiston
Mill

Preston Vale

2

WALK 24 ;
PENKRIDGE

0   ½   1

km

Station

Riverside Farm

A449 (T)

START
Littleton Arms

1

Penkridge

The Walk

1. From the Littleton Arms, turn right to the main road and then turn left to walk out of the centre across the bridge. Go under the railway bridge and left again along a quiet No Through Road in approximately 100 metres. Follow this quiet lane for well over a mile to the farm complex at Preston Vale.

2. As you approach the farm, cross the stile and head right, as signposted, for the Staffordshire Way. Follow the field boundary ahead and then at the corner go left to continue along the boundary to cross a track and by a small group of willow trees. Go right at the protruding corner and follow the boundary to a stile and road.

3. Go left and the lane soon meets a junction near Mitton. Turn left again to cross a stream and walk up to a triangular junction. Keep ahead across it to walk up a track to a large field. Walk ahead to a corner of a wood and at the far end a clear path cuts right across a field to a gap in the next boundary. Walk down to Bickford Meadows.

4. Bickford Meadows is an area of wet grassland managed by the Staffordshire Wildlife Trust. It attracts a rich variety of birds and water loving plants. Cross the footbridge and walk up to a junction where the Staffordshire Way bears right through the meadow. You however keep left to walk up a bridleway to a road.

5. Turn left along the road to walk into the hamlet of Whiston, passing by Pear Tree farm and a number of attractive cottages. On reaching a T-junction go right to pass by The White Swan (which was closed at the time of writing but will hopefully be re open now). Continue along the road to approach the entrance on the left to Whiston Mill. Before this is a little path on the left which runs between hedges to a gate.

6. Cross it and head slightly right to a footbridge over the Whiston Brook and onward to the right of buildings at Preston Vale. On reaching the road, go right to retrace your steps back into Penkridge.

25. Seighford

Route: Seighford – Clanford Covert – Seighford Church – Floss Bridge – Cooksland – Seighford

Distance: 4 miles (6.5km)

Map: OS Pathfinder 850 Stafford

Start: The Hollybush Inn, Seighford

Access: Seighford is best approached from the B5405 at Great Bridgeford. There is a small amount of car parking in the village. There is also a bus service from Stafford on Mondays to Saturdays.

The Hollybush Inn. 01785 282280

The Hollybush is an extensive pub with small bar to front, and large lounge bar to the rear. The most impressive corner is the inglenook fireplace. There is also a restaurant and tables on patio facing the car park. The original part of the pub dates back to 1675 and is best described as being adorned with lots of original bric-a-brac. Lord Lichfield was turned away by a previous licensee for wearing jeans and no tie! Joe Brown and his brothers were turned away for having collar length hair but be assured that ramblers are welcome! Usual opening times are 12pm – 2.30pm and 6pm – 11pm. Food is served all days from 12pm – 2pm and 6pm – 9.30pm. Families are welcome. On handpull are Ansells Mild, Tetley bitter and Marstons Pedigree.

Seighford

Not far from Stafford is the small village of Seighford, where cottages and farmhouses line one main street leading to the impressive church. Its 18th Century Gothic-style tower and clock face beckon the passer-by and a closer inspection reveals an interior which dates from medieval times. At the other end for the village is the imposing half-timbered Seighford Hall, built in the 16th Century, but with several 19th Century additions. It was a family home for centuries, then became a hotel, and is now a home for the elderly. The curious-looking brick building which stands alongside looks like a chapel, but was, in fact, built as a gamekeeper's cottage.

A sinking feeling at Seighford

The Walk

1. Start the figure-of-eight walk from the Hollybush Inn. Turn left to walk through the village. At the T-junction at the end of the street, go left and at the next junction turn left again, signposted to Haughton and Derrington.

2. This winds around to the old Seighford airfield, which now sees learner drivers of heavy goods vehicles testing their skills, rather than pilots and planes. Just after crossing the tarmac strip, and before Clanford Covert, go left over a stile to enter a level field. Keep ahead along the boundary, which curves left to a stile in the corner. Cross it and continue ahead to the next stile by wooden bars. Keep ahead through fields with a fence or hedge to your left until you reach a track. Go left to walk along the track and, on reaching the road, go left to return to the village.

3. If you wish to complete the second half of the loop, turn right after the entrance to the church (opposite the school). Follow the lane down to a ford, where the waters of Gamesley Brook swirl across the road. Fortunately, there is a little brick footbridge spanning the water for pedestrians. Once across, go right along a well-worn bridleway. This soon curves left to run alongside woodland known as Moor Covert and continues towards the railway at Floss Bridge.

4. At the T-junction beforehand, go left and climb gently along an equally pleasant bridle route to a minor road. Go left immediately to cross a stile here and head slightly right through the field. Cross another two fields and stiles, maintaining a similar direction, to reach a stile which exits onto a lane.

5. Go left for a few paces and then turn right over a stile by a gate. Walk ahead to a stile above a brook. Bear slightly right to a footbridge and once over, climb up to a stile by a gate and through a gate just beyond. The path keeps ahead between renovated farm buildings to a road in the village. The Hollybush is nearby.

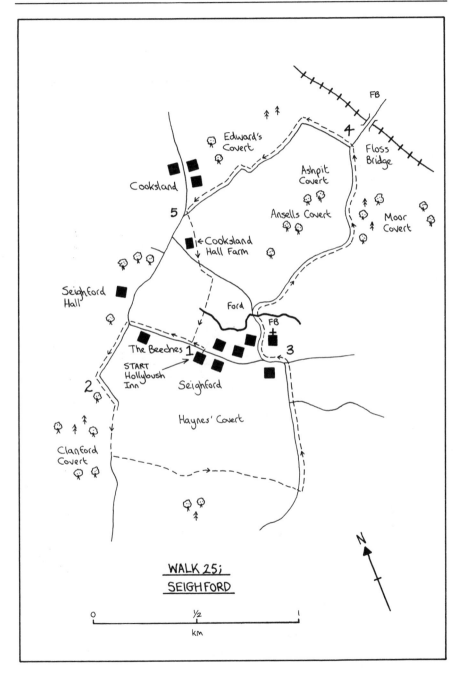

WALK 25;
SEIGHFORD

0   ½   1
                    km

```
┌─────────────────────────────────────────────────────┐
│                                                       │
│              26. Shenstone                            │
│                                                       │
└─────────────────────────────────────────────────────┘
```

Route: Shenstone – Footherley Hall – Moor Lane – Footherley Lane – Hollyhill Lane – Shenstone

Distance: 4 miles (7km)

Map: OS Pathfinder 892 Lichfield & Brownhills

Start: Shenstone Railway Station

Access: There is a daily rail service from Birmingham and Lichfield. Shenstone is off the A5127 from Lichfield. There is parking near to the railway station.

The Railway. 01543 480503

This village pub, which is obviously a stone's throw from the railway, was previously a butcher's shop and an old chapel. The pub has several bar areas and an outdoor garden. In summer it seems as if the pub is in bloom for the hanging baskets offer a profusion of colour. No wonder the Railway has been the winner of the 'Best Garden' competition in past years. Usually open all day every day if busy otherwise Monday to Thursday hours restricted to 12pm – 4pm and 5pm – 11pm. A full range of meals is available from 12pm – 2.30pm and 6pm – 10pm. Families are welcome, especially in the garden where there is a pets' corner and barbecue. On handpull and in good condition are Marstons' Pedigree Bitter, Brewer's Choice guest beers and Banks's Mild. Another pub to look out for is The Bull's Head, as it houses the original Court Room where petty sessions would have been held; no doubt a good time was had by all except those before the bench.

Shenstone

Shenstone is derived from Seneste, or Scenestan, meaning shining stone which refers to the red sandstone. Nearby is the site of a Roman farmstead and the route of Ryknild Street. Several artefacts have been found in the past when fields have been ploughed or foundations dug for houses. Shenstone is predominantly a 20th century dormitory community but the old quarter includes several buildings from the 17th to 19th centuries. The church is perhaps of greatest interest. It stands on a hill, about five minutes walk from the Railway pub, and has two church towers. One is a ruined tower, being the remains from a medieval church, and the other belongs to the much restored Victorian church. Shenstone Court stands near to the railway and not far from the walk. It was originally owned once by Sir Richard Cooper, a vet who became MP for Walsall. He invented 'Cooper's sheep dip' but was also responsible for planting the beautiful avenues of trees in the village. When walking around Shenstone look for two houses in New Road called 'Defiance' and 'Victory'. These names relate to a case some years ago when a gentleman went to the High Court as neighbours had objected to his building plans. Obviously, he won his case!

The Railway at Shenstone

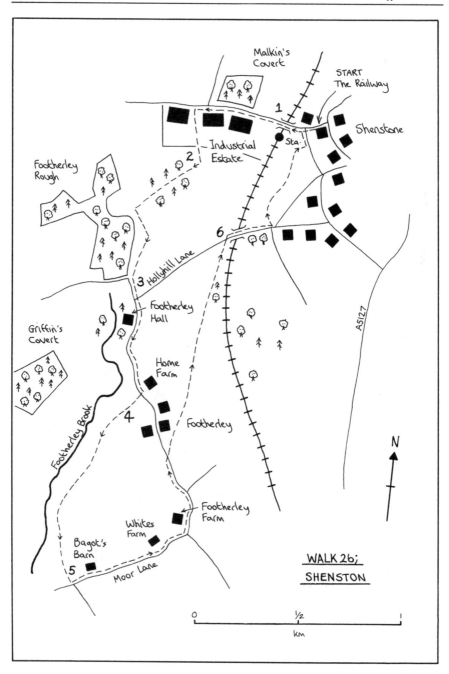

Malkin's
Covert

START
The Railway

1

Shenstone

Sta.

Industrial
Estate

2

Footherley
Rough

6

3 Hollyhill Lane

Footherley
Hall

Griffin's
Covert

Home
Farm

4

Footherley

Footherley Brook

A5127

N

Footherley
Farm

Whites
Farm

Bagot's
Barn

5

Moor Lane

WALK 26;
SHENSTON

0   ½   1
km

The Walk

1. Start from the station. Go left over the bridge. You will see a pumping station to the right, which dates from 1891. Keep ahead by industrial premises and 200 metres beyond. Look for a footpath (signed) on left which runs between security fences.

2. The path enters a very large field of beet where you go left. Cross the footbridge and then go right. Follow the path to a wood known as Fotherley Rough. Towards the top corner look for a gap in the hedge on the right. This cuts through the wood to the road.

3. Go left to pass Footherley Hall and then look for Home Farm. Go right over a stile here into a field and walk towards another stile. Cross it and keep ahead. The field often is sown with cereal but the path is clear as it heads towards a field corner where you join Ryknild Street. It is hard to believe that this would have been a major Roman thoroughfare.

4. Cross the stile guarding the footbridge, then head slightly right across the field and cross the stile beneath a tree. Now keep company with the hedge on the left. At the next boundary, cross a stile and keep left again. Go through a gate to exit onto a track.

5. Go left to follow the track by an old farmhouse. Keep ahead along the lane passing by Whites Farm and meeting Footherley Lane where Footherley Farm stands to the left. The road bends left and passes by a group of houses. Be vigilant as the stile on the left is not clear but the path is. You can see Shenstone church as a landmark. Head slightly left. Cross the stile at the next boundary and go ahead. There is now a very large field with very sandy soil, often with cereal crop, but well walked so there is no problem.

6. The path runs through a pocket of woodland and ahead to a lane. Go right and over the railway. Continue to a junction and where you turn left for the railway station and the Railway pub.

27. Stafford

Route: Stafford – Greenway – Derrington – Stafford Castle – Stafford

Distance: 3 miles (5km)

Map: OS Pathfinder 850 Stafford

Start: The Stafford Arms, Stafford

Access: There are trains from Wolverhampton and Stoke-on-Trent. Stafford is situated on the A34 road from Stoke-on-Trent. There are several car parks.

The Stafford Arms. 01785 53313

Voted CAMRA Stafford & Stone Pub of the Year 1994, the Stafford Arms offers Titanic Best bitter, stout, Captain Smith's, Lifeboat and four guest beers. Its attractions include two beer festivals a year and corridor skittles in summer. There is reputed to be a gold krugerand buried in concrete in the cellar for good luck when the building was refurbished as a public house. Usual opening times are all day on Mondays to Saturdays. Lunches are served 12pm – 2pm, Monday to Sunday. Evening meals are from 5pm – 7pm, Monday to Friday. Families are welcome. There are a few seats outside but no garden.

Stafford

The name Stafford is derived from 'staithford' meaning a ford by the landing place. There are many fine buildings in the town, including the Shire Hall, a proud Georgian building. Many other 18th and early 19th century houses can be seen throughout the town. Best known is the Ancient High House which dates from 1555. It is thought to be the largest timber-framed town house in England, and now houses the visitor centre and museum.

Stafford has always been a good town to explore on foot, perhaps from the steps of the Ancient High House. There are also several local countryside walks which can be easily reached from the historic core without too much road walking. Two such walks, to Doxey Marshes and Stafford Castle, have been included in a new booklet "Walking in Stafford Borough" which features 14 local walks in the area.

The Walk

1. Start your walk from Stafford railway station. Turn left and left again to pass The Stafford Arms. At the end of this road, turn left to walk along Railway Street to a junction by the Railway Inn. Go left over the bridge and descend by a works and car park to a kissing gate and new road where houses are being built nearby.

Stafford Castle: see instruction (5)

2. Go right and follow the road verge to a dead end where you join a narrow tarmac lane. Bear left along it until you reach a bend just before Burleyfields farm. Go right to join The Greenway, a route for cyclists, walkers and horseriders using the trackbed of a railway which operated from the late 1850s until 1964.

3. Turn left then follow the trail under the motorway. After the next small brick bridge, go left down the embankment to a lane. Turn

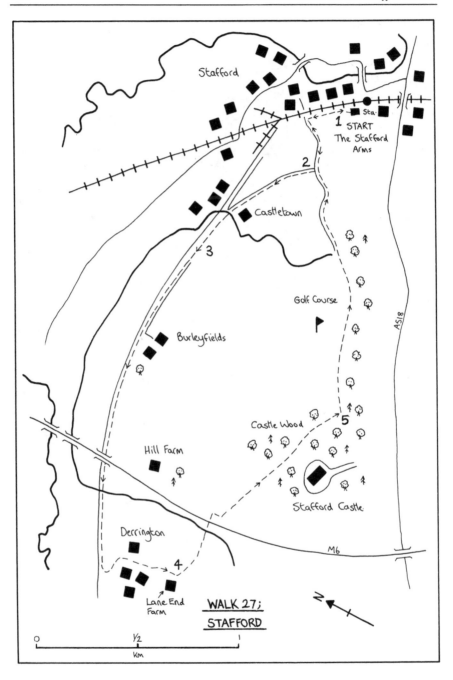

Stafford

Castletown

Burleyfields

Golf Course

Castle Wood

Hill Farm

Stafford Castle

Derrington

Lane End
Farm

Sta.

1 START
The Stafford
Arms

2

3

5

4

M6

A518

WALK 27;
STAFFORD

0   ½   1
          Km

right to walk towards the houses of Derrington and you catch a glimpse of a small sandstone chapel. Cut left at the corner to cross a footbridge and stile into a field. Go right to walk ahead to the next boundary. Cross a stile and continue ahead along the field's edge. At the end of the field cross a stile and turn left.

4. The path leads to a tunnel under the motorway then rises up to a field. Cross a stile, and follow a well-worn path through the middle of the field. Cross another stile and walk along the hedgerow. As this bends left, keep ahead to cross a stile in the next boundary. Stafford castle stands to your right, dating originally from medieval times but having been rebuilt as a dwelling in later centuries. The fascinating story of the castle and how it has been saved for posterity is told at the visitor centre.

5. If visiting the castle, keep to the right along the periphery of the castle grounds to a stile and join the entrance road. Otherwise, head slightly left to a stile. Go over this and follow a clear track alongside the entire length of the golf course, thought at one time to be part of a medieval deer park associated with the castle. The path eventually gives out to a modern estate road. Cross it and walk along the little metalled path to the next road. Cross over to the kissing gate and retrace your steps back to the Stafford Arms.

```
┌─────────────────────────────────────────────────────────┐
│  ┌───────────────────────────────────────────────────┐  │
│  │                                                     │  │
│  │              28. Tamworth                           │  │
│  │                                                     │  │
│  └───────────────────────────────────────────────────┘  │
└─────────────────────────────────────────────────────────┘
```

Route: Tamworth – River Tame – Birmingham and Fazeley Canal – Dunstall Lane – Tamworth

Distance: 4½ miles (7km)

Map: OS Pathfinders 893 Tamworth and 892 Lichfield and Brownhills

Start: Lady Bridge, Tamworth

Access: Tamworth is well served by bus and train.

The Market Vaults. 01827 69653

The Market Vaults is a listed building, one of the oldest in Tamworth, and has a half timbered wall in passage leading a rear beer garden. There are tales of a ghost in the pub as things do disappear and re-appear for no reason, but be assured that this friendly town-centre pub welcomes walkers. Usual opening times: Monday to Thursday, 11pm – 3pm and 6pm – 11pm. It is open all day Friday and Saturday. Lunches are served Tuesday to Saturday 12pm – 3.30pm. Families are welcome. On handpull are Banks's Mild and Bitter, plus Camerons Strongarm.

Tamworth

Tamworth's rich heritage reflects the strong influence of the Saxons and Normans. It was the home to several Saxon Kings and evidence suggests that it fast became the capital of the Kingdom of Mercia. The Normans realised the importance of the settlement and the magnificent shell of the castle remains defiantly to this day. Set on a bluff above riverside grounds, this ancient fortress houses an exhibition about life in Norman times. There are also several period rooms, dating from later centuries, one of which is said to be haunted. Earliest reference to the town was in a charter signed by Offa, King of Mercia, in AD 781. Ethelfleda, daughter of Alfred the

The rear of the Three Tuns on the canalside at Tamworth

Great, was thought to have built a stockade here in her fight against the Danes, and in 926 a mint was established. In more recent times, two eminent figures associated with the town are Sir Robert Peel, founder of the police force, and Thomas Guy, founder of Guy's Hospital in London. In 1700 he built Tamworth's Town Hall. In front of the building there is a statue of Sir Robert Peel.

The Walk

1. The walk follows the waters of the River Tame but be warned – it can get wet in places. From the castle, walk to the pedestrian-only Lady Bridge. At the far end of the bridge, go right on a path which heads slightly left away from the river towards a footpath post at the end of a hedge. It then curves right again under a concrete bridge to continue along the bank of a flood relief channel of the Tame.

2. Follow this channel to a point beyond the paper mill, seen across

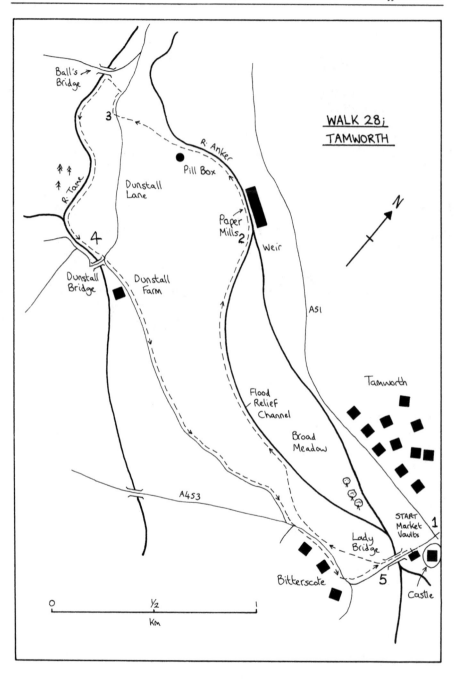

WALK 28;
TAMWORTH

the weir on the opposite bank. The path continues along as the river bends left then begins to curve right. Pass by a pill box and you will know that it is time to head slightly left across a rough pasture towards a hedge. The path is not clear but there is a telecommunication tower in the background which provides a landmark. Walk beneath the electricity wires through an area of marshy ground so pick out your path carefully.

3. You reach a gate where there is a stile just to the right. This exits onto a road. Turn right and when you are around the first corner go through a gate on the left (signposted). Head across the field on a well-worn path to an awkward stile which leads onto the towpath of the Birmingham and Fazely canal.

4. Turn left to follow this pleasant waterway towards Tamworth until you reach Dunstall Bridge where you rise up to the road. Go left to follow this narrow lane back to town, exiting as it bends sharp right by houses to a large roundabout. Cross on the left with extreme and then take the turning on the left, Bone Hill Road, which runs back to Lady Bridge. Simply head in the direction of the castle.

5. Tamworth has many attractions, a pedestrianised shopping area and a town trail which guides you through the historic parts of the town.

29. Trysull

Route: Wombourne – The Bratch – Trysull – Awbridge – Wombourne

Distance: 3½ miles (6.5km)

Map: OS Pathfinder 912 Wolverhampton (South)

Start: Wombourne Railway Station

Access: Wombourne is well served by buses from Wolverhampton. There is a stop five minutes from Wombourne old station. Wombourne is situated just off the A449 road, south of Wolverhampton. There is parking at the old station.

The Bell Inn. 01902 892871

Unusually for this area, the Bell is a Holden's house serving fine ales from the Woodsetton brewery. It also sells Batham's bitter. This is a well-appointed public house in a lovely location and which is popular with local people. Standing next to the church it is not surprising that it is known as The Bell. Most of the current building is 18th century but it is thought that there has been a basic ale house and inn on the site for many centuries. The inn contains an interesting history of what it was like to be a publican in the last century; many brewed their own beer and worked an 18-hour day, from 4am to 10pm, in order to combine brewing with running the pub. Fortunately for us, Holden's secured the pub from Bass in 1993. Usual opening times: 11.30pm – 3pm and 5.30pm – 11pm, Monday to Saturday. Children welcome into the restaurant during the day and up to 7.30pm at night. There are also three patio areas.

Trysull

This is a quiet village where milling once was a major occupation but no longer. The old mill still stands on the edge of Smestow Brook, machinery and wheel preserved, but is now converted into

Trysull church

a private house. You pass near it on the walk. There are a number of impressive houses here such as The Croft – a late Georgian house of red brick, built in the early 1800s by 'Gentleman Perry', whose tomb is by the south door of the church. The Manor dates from the mid 17th century and it is said that Dr Johnson's aunt lived here. An inscription on the porch reads;

> *Stranger, should this catch your eye*
> *Do a favour, passing by*
> *Bless this house.*

The church of All Saints dates from the 12th century and is much loved in the community. One amusing tale is that there was a bequest that the verger should be paid £1 per year to keep the congregation awake during sermons.

The Walk

1. Start at Wombourne old railway station. Go down the entrance to Bratch Lane. Turn right to walk up to Bratch Locks. The road passes a waterworks and small picnic site. It then rises to a group of houses known as The Bratch. Turn left into Bratch Common Road.

2. Pass the turn for the farm, and then look for a stile on the right. Cross it and head slightly right across the field to another stile. Continue along the field edge, then cross a stile on the left by a gate. You may see cricket being played on the pitch to the right. Now keep company with the hedge on the right.

3. On reaching the lane, turn right. Drop down to cross a bridge. Pass the cottage and private drive, then cross the stile by a gate on the right. The way is not entirely clear in this field but head slightly right up the field, then bear left over the brow. You are aiming for the top-left, far corner. Cross the stile, and go as directed by the waymarker post

4. Enter the village of Trysull. The Plough pub is to your left but turn right to the main junction in the village by the church. The Bell is on the other side of the church.

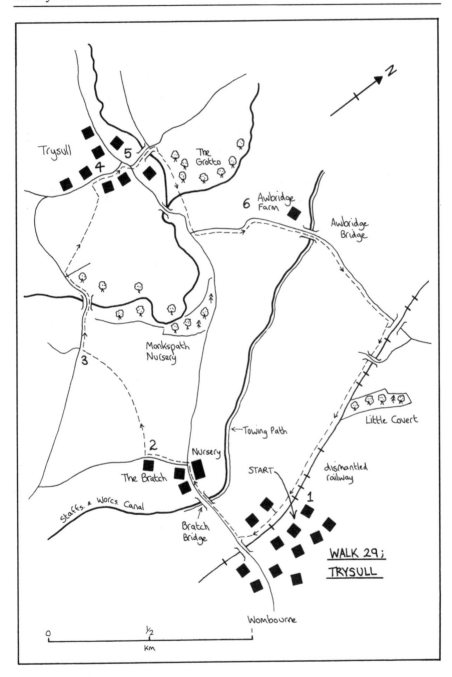

Trysull

5

4

The Grotto

6 Awbridge Farm

Awbridge Bridge

Monkspath Nursery

3

Little Covert

2

Nursery

Towing Path

dismantled railway

The Bratch

START

1

Staffs. & Worcs. Canal

Bratch Bridge

WALK 29;
TRYSULL

Wombourne

0   ½
Km

5. At the church, go right and then left into Holloway. Walk over the bridge, where you will see Mill House on the left. You, however, turn right over a stile by the entrance to a drive and walk through a wood ahead, with a stream to the right. Cross the stile by a gate to exit into a field. Cross the stile beneath the treesand go ahead along field and first right to exit onto road.

6. Go left and walk up past a farm, then onwards to another and Awbridge Bridge. Go over the canal and at the next junction bear right to walk along the road until you meet the old railway track. Rise up to it and go left towards Wombourne station which at one time was part of the Great Western Railway system from Wolver- hampton to Kingswinford. It is now a tearoom. It is less than a mile away.

30. Yoxall

Route: Yoxall – River Swarbourn – Woodhouses – Bond End – Yoxall

Distance: 2½ miles (4km)

Map: OS Pathfinder 872 Rugely and Lichfield

Start: The Crown, Yoxall

Access: Yoxall is served by buses from Burton upon Trent. Travel on the A515 to the village, but there is only limited on street parking.

The Crown. 01543 472551

The Crown is a good looking village pub which stands on the main street. This cheerful hostelry gained entry into the Good Beer Guide in 1996 an it serves a rather good pint of Marston's Pedigree. Usual opening times are Monday to Friday, 11.30pm – 3pm and 5.30pm – 11pm. Saturday and Sunday: all day. Walk through the impressive front door to enter the bar or the lounge. The latter includes an eating area by a magnificent fireplace. There is a limited menu available at lunchtimes but please note that there is no food on Sunday. Families are welcome in the conservatory area.

Yoxall

Yoxall is an unusual name. It was originally part of the Bishop of Chester's lands, and is featured in the Domesday Book as 'Locheshale' meaning 'land ploughed by a yoke of oxen'. Since those times, Yoxall has remained a rural community not reached by canal or railway. The River Swarbourn, also, has never been navigable. As a result, many of the earlier houses and buildings have survived and much of the village is designated as a conservation area, nestled around the splendid parish church of St Peter. The 17th century grange was once the rectory. Another interesting building is the three-storey house, The Hollies, which was a tape mill until the last

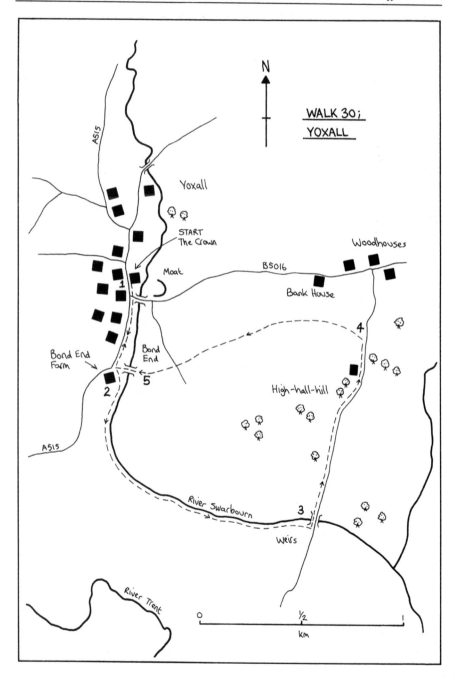

N

WALK 30;
YOXALL

A515

Yoxall

START
The Crown

Woodhouses

BS016

Bank House

Moat

1

Bond End
Farm

Bond
End

5

2

4

High-hall-hill

A515

River Swarbourn

3

Weirs

River Trent

0   ½   1
km

century. You might also notice Birmingham House which is an early 17th century timber-framed house. It was the home of George Walton, the grandfather of Izaac Walton. There are so many fine houses in the village.

The Walk

1. From the entrance to The Crown, turn right to walk along the main street in the direction of Lichfield. Notice Armsons Antiques of Yoxall on your right. At a corner, as main road bends right, cross over to go ahead along a narrow path. It is signposted to Meadow Lane.

2. The path runs between houses and into a field by the river. Cross the track to the sewage works, then soon go over a stile beneath elderberry and hawthorn before bearing left to follow the river, lined with alder, reeds and smelling sweet with rosebay willowherb.

3. Follow the river until you reach a stile by a gate. Rise up to the road and turn left to walk towards a group of dwellings known as Woodhouses. Pass a farm at High-hall hill standing to your left. Just beyond there are gates and a track on the right. At the end of the fencing go over a ditch to enter the field.

4. Head slightly right up towards a small pool, with a hedge/fence to the right. Go left to cut through the field corner the gap ahead. Cross a stile into field usually sown with corn. Head slightly left and midfield pass to the right of trees and then slightly left. There is a landmark, a thatched cottage and farm across the field to the right. You are heading in the direction of Rugeley Power station which can be seen in the distance. Follow the line of two oaks to a stile in the hedge beyond.

5. Keep slightly left and cross the ditch by the poles. There is no stile as such! Continue ahead to cross the next stile. There is an option here, you can go right up the track, or simply continue along the little path ahead.

Yoxall church

THE BEST PUB WALKS...across the UK!

Join in the fun ... explore the most scenic parts of Britain with these attractive, reliable walking guides. Each one features easy walks, wonderful scenery, plus plenty of background information to add interest – and naturally they all include pubs that welcome walkers!

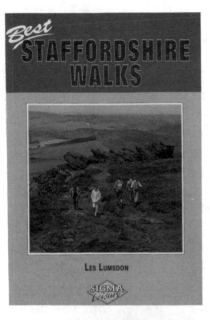